AN ORDINARY SIGNALMAN

By
John Dawson

Published by

MELROSE BOOKS

An Imprint of Melrose Press Limited
St Thomas Place, Ely
Cambridgeshire
CB7 4GG, UK
www.melrosebooks.com

FIRST EDITION

Copyright © John Dawson 2008

The Author asserts his moral right to
be identified as the author of this work

Cover designed by Matt Stephens

ISBN 978 1 906561 04 8

All rights reserved. No part of this publication may be reproduced,
stored in a retrieval system, or transmitted, in any form or by any means
electronic, mechanical, photocopying, recording or otherwise,
without the prior permission of the publishers.

This book is sold subject to the condition that it shall not,
by way of trade or otherwise, be lent, re-sold, hired out or
otherwise circulated without the publisher's prior consent
in any form of binding or cover other than that in which
it is published and without a similar condition including this
condition being imposed on the subsequent purchaser.

Printed and bound in Great Britain by:
Biddles, King's Lynn, Norfolk

CONTENTS

Introduction and Background vii
    The Ships viii
    Shore Bases x

THE DIARY – PART I
In which I am never far from England xi
    1: The First Few Days 1
    2: Training, Barracks and the First Sea-Going Ship 3
    3: Disillusionment and the Toughening Up Process 16
    4: HMCS *Ottawa* 17
    5: HMS Forth – July 1941–1943 19
        Part 1: In St John's, Newfoundland and a Trip to the USA 19
        Part 2: An Uneventful Convoy, Home and our New Job 22
        Part 3: My Work, Impressions and How Conscience Overcame Security 31
    6: Leave, Barracks and a First Glimpse of Cruisers (HMS *Spartan*) 68
    7: Home Fleet, But Not For Long?? 71

THE DIARY – PART II
In which I leave the shores of England for 25 months of adventure 73
    8: Mediterranean, Here We Come 75
    9: The Waiting Period, Christmas at Sea, Then a Flagship 77
    10: Prelude to Action 79
    11: Minturno and Anzio 80
    12: The End of the *Spartan* (1905 Hours, 29th Jan 1944) 83
    13: Unlucky For Some, But Not For All 87
    14: Recuperation, and a Big Disappointment 89
    15: Algiers, Malta and a Fresh Hope Shattered 94
    16: HMS *Aurora* March 21st 1944 – Nov 16th 1945. Docking, Working Up,
        But a Happier Ship 96

CONTENTS (cont.)

17: Palermo, Review by the King, and Routine (?) Work 99
18: South of France, and Toulon 101
19: Five Eventful Months in the Aegean. Sept 1944 – Jan 1945 106
20: From Action to Passenger Ship 124
21: I Become a Yeoman, and Genoa Makes Me Work for a Living 127
22: Trouble in Syria, and a Welcome Refit 134
23: Four Months in Malta and Cricket 136
24: Working Up Again, A Cruise, And Good-Bye, *Aurora* 139
25: The Last Episodes, Before Becoming Mr Dawson 142

This book is dedicated to my father John, mother Mollie and sister Pat, and also to Auntie Eileen, to whom the letters were written.

Thanks to my wife Caroline who typed the manuscript and encouraged me throughout, and to Auntie Eileen who answered many questions about the characters referred to in the letters.
Thanks also to all at Melrose Books who have been so helpful.

John Dawson soon after joining up in January 1941.

INTRODUCTION AND BACKGROUND

John Dawson, my Dad, died on 3rd May 1986 at the age of 64 from a sudden heart attack. He was due to retire following his 65th birthday on 27th August 1986.

It was ironic that he died on Rugby League Cup Final day, as following Leeds Rugby League team and Yorkshire cricket were his major interests as I recall them. Indeed, as soon as I could walk, he took me to Headingley to watch Leeds Rugby. We lived in Headingley, about 15 minutes' walk from the ground.

The Dawsons were a close family. We lived at 7 Cliff Lane, and my grandparents on my father's side lived at 9 Cliff Lane. A great uncle and great aunt were at 11 Cliff Lane. All the family at that time lived in the Headingley area.

Dad had an elder sister and brother, Eileen and Sydney. Sydney died in late 2006, but Eileen is still alive, living in Headingley.

Apart from sport, Dad's main interests were the Church – he was Church Secretary at Blenheim Baptist Church in Leeds for a number of years – and his business, which was the family business of Dawson & Son Ltd, formerly called John Dawson & Son. In one guise or another, the firm had been in existence since 1868. It was only sold out of the family in 2005, when the current Directors realised that there was no one to take over when they retired, and sold to a Dutch family.

Dad was the only one of his family at the time to join the forces in the Second World War. In the year before he died, he sat down and talked about some of the events that he experienced, and I shall refer to these later. However, for many years I have read more than once the 'Diary' that he wrote up between January and March 1946.

That Diary he called 'My Experiences and Thoughts in the Navy, December 1940 to January 1946'.

He began with the following words: 'The views expressed in this spontaneous account, as authentic as memory allows, are completely my own, written for my own amusement in later life.' However, in his chats to me during his last year, Dad said that he would be happy for me to write this up once he had died, albeit he did not anticipate dying quite so soon.

Subsequently, when my Auntie Eileen moved out of her house on St Michaels Lane, Headingley, alongside the rugby and cricket grounds, to a smaller property in 1999, she found a large number of the letters that Dad had written to her as his big sister during the war, and these will also be set out in what follows.

Dad had been brought up in a pretty strict Baptist family, where his father was very active in Leeds and Yorkshire Baptist circles. This strength of belief and faith comes out in many of the comments made in the Diary.

What I intend to achieve is to set out the Diary as it was written, but link in some of the letters that Dad sent to his sister Eileen, and also seek to set the scene by narrating what was happening in the war during the period described in the Diary.

Occasional errors of spelling, grammar and punctuation in the original Diary have been corrected here, but otherwise the text is unaltered. The letters, as primary historical documents, are reproduced exactly as they were written.

THE SHIPS
HMS *FORTH*

The *Forth* was built by John Brown & Co at Clydebank. She was launched on 11th August 1938 and completed on 14th May 1939. She served with 2nd Submarine Flotilla from 1939 to 1941, based at Dundee, Rosyth and then Holy Loch. In February 1941, she crossed the Atlantic for a short period, operating submarines from Halifax, Nova Scotia, where they were used to protect convoys against surface raiders. For a short period she maintained A/S vessels and then reverted to S/M support. The 3rd and 2nd Submarine Flotillas combined from December 1941 and *Forth* remained at Holy Loch until 1945 and at Rothesay from 1945 to 1947. She continued in service for a number of years until her name was changed in February 1972 to *Defiance*. She was finally placed on the disposal list in 1978 and on 25th July 1985 she arrived to be scrapped on the Medway, Kent, after 47 years' service.

HMS *SPARTAN*

The *Spartan* was a Dido class cruiser of 5770 tons of standard displacement with a main armament of eight 5.25-inch guns. She was built and engined by Vickers Armstrong of Barrow. She was ordered on 4th September 1939 and laid down on 21st December the same year. Work was suspended for a time but the contract was confirmed in February 1942 and the job was restarted. The *Spartan* was launched on 27th August 1942 and completed for service with the Royal Navy on 10th August 1943.

She was commissioned with a Devonport crew under the command of Captain P V McLaughlin. She was originally intended for service with the Eastern Fleet, but after a couple of months with the Home Fleet, she was despatched to the Mediterranean. She arrived in Malta on 28th October 1943 to be temporarily attached to the Mediterranean Fleet. She went on to Taranto to join the 15th Cruiser Squadron on 8th November.

In the early evening of 29th January 1944, while on duty off Anzio, the *Spartan* was hit by a radio-controlled bomb and an hour later she had to be abandoned. Five officers and 41 ratings were posted killed or missing presumed killed, and 42 ratings were wounded.

HMS *AURORA*

The *Aurora* was an Arethusa class cruiser; she was built by Portsmouth Dockyard. The keel was laid down 27th July 1935 and she was launched on 20th August 1936. She was commissioned on 12th November 1937 and decommissioned in April 1946. Subsequently she was sold to the Chinese Navy and re-named.

The standard displacement was 5270 tons. She carried three six-inch dual guns.

She served with the Home Fleet from completion and saw much active service there. She then transferred in the autumn of 1941 to the Mediterranean.

On 19th December 1941, while on her way to intercept an Italian convoy bound for Tripoli, she and other ships ran into a newly laid Italian minefield. She was badly damaged. She was patched up at Malta before sailing home on 29th March 1942 for full repair at Liverpool, which took until the end of June 1942. While she was in Malta, the ship's crew heard that the City of Bradford (in Yorkshire) had adopted the *Aurora*. She was visited by the Lord Mayor while in Liverpool.

She returned to the Mediterranean and again saw much active service. She participated in the invasion of Sicily and the Salerno landings before moving into the Aegean in October 1943. There she was damaged by bombs and withdrew to Taranto for repairs, a task which lasted until April 1944. In August 1944 she was at the landings in the south of France and then returned to the Aegean, where she assisted in the liberation of Athens.

HMS *SHERWOOD*

The *Sherwood* was a destroyer of the Town class. She was commissioned on 23rd October 1940, having been transferred from the United States with other destroyers in exchange for bases in the Western Hemisphere.

Her previous name had been the USS *John Rodgers*. She had been laid down on 25th September 1918 and launched on 26th April 1919. She was commissioned in the US Navy on 22nd July 1919 and de-commissioned on

23rd October 1940. Her displacement was 1190 tons. The de-commissioning and commissioning had taken place while the ship was at Halifax, Nova Scotia. She sailed to the United Kingdom on 1st November 1940. On 18th November she arrived at Belfast and continued on to Portsmouth. After an overhaul, she sailed to join the 12th Escort Group, Western Approaches Command, at Londonderry, Northern Ireland. She transferred with her group to Iceland in April 1941 and was involved with the hunt for *Bismarck*. During the summer she underwent repairs in the Clyde and then returned to Londonderry, from where she operated into the New Year of 1942.

After various problems and the need for repairs, she was taken out of active service at Chatham in September 1943. She was stripped of all useable parts and ordnance and towed to the Humber, where she was beached in shallow water and used as an aircraft target. Her hulk was scrapped in 1945.

HMCS *OTTAWA*

The *Ottawa* began life in 1931 as HMS *Crusader* before she was commissioned into the Royal Canadian Navy on 15th June 1938 in Chatham, England. Following the outbreak of the Second World War, she was stationed at Halifax, Nova Scotia, where she escorted convoys between Great Britain and Canada.

In the first year of the war, the *Ottawa* conducted convoy escort duties in the Atlantic. In autumn 1940, she was deployed to Scotland to assist in local escort operations until her return to Canada in spring 1941. She then joined the Newfoundland Escort Force, with which she continued her service off the coast of Newfoundland until her loss 15 months later.

On the night of 13th/14th September 1942, near Newfoundland, she was torpedoed and some 30 minutes later she was hit a second time. She sank, and five officers and 109 men were lost. There were only 65 survivors.

SHORE BASES
HMS *ROYAL ARTHUR*

The *Royal Arthur* was one of several assessment camps where new recruits were assessed, kitted out and sent to various depots. Thousands went through these camps. Before the war, HMS *Royal Arthur* had been a Butlins Holiday Camp at Skegness, and after the war she was reverted back to that.

HMS *DRAKE*

Drake was the Naval Barracks at Devonport. The barracks suffered from the air raids on that area and, in particular, on the night of Monday/Tuesday 21st/22nd April 1941, 113 people were killed in an air raid when the whole of Devonport suffered badly.

THE DIARY

PART I

In which I am never far from England

Cover of first of 3 notebooks forming the Diary written in 1946.

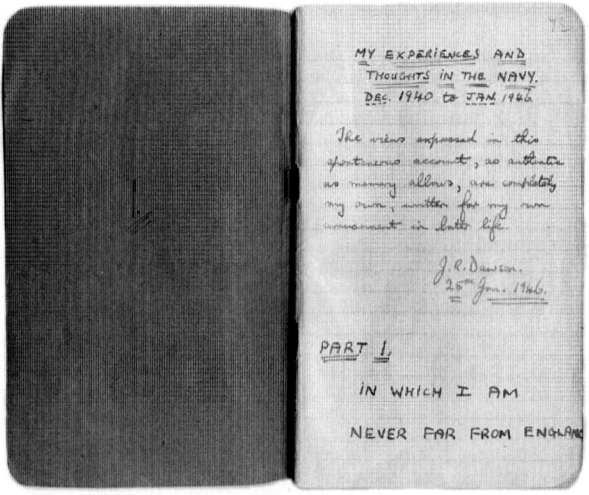

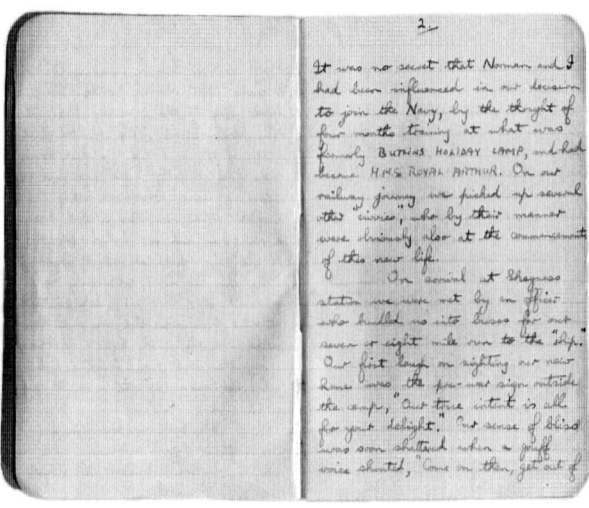

Opening pages of the Diary.

1

THE FIRST FEW DAYS

1940

On Tuesday morning 17th December 1940, Norman Brooks and I went along to the Recruiting Office in New Station Street, Leeds, on the first stage of the new life we had chosen, more from loyalty and conscience than desire. We were feeling confident that our decision had been the right one and we looked forward to the new experiences which would be coming our way, collectively and individually. Our only disappointment at that time was that we had been called up the week before Christmas, surely the most popular festive and religious season of the year to any man.

We had our preliminary instructions before entraining for Skegness, where we were to report. It was no secret that Norman and I had been influenced in our decision to join the Navy, by the thought of 4 months' training at what was formerly Butlins Holiday Camp, and had become HMS *Royal Arthur*. On our railway journey we picked up several other 'civvies', who by their manner were obviously also at the commencement of this new life.

On arrival at Skegness station we were met by an officer who bundled us into buses for our seven or eight mile run to the 'ship'. Our first laugh on sighting our new home was the pre-war sign outside the camp, 'Our true intent is all for your delight.' Our sense of bliss was soon shattered when a gruff voice shouted, "Come on then, get out of it." We were bundled once again, this time to a dining hall where we had a typical naval tea of bread and butter with a sprinkling of jam. We then heard our first naval 'buzz', which to the ignorant civilian means nothing, but we were told that the Navy lived on 'buzzes'. The word quite simply means rumour, and in later years I found that whilst there was a buzz there was always hope, especially when abroad. Anyway our first buzz was that we would be going home in 2 days' time for 10 days' Christmas leave. We thought this was a weak joke and none of us took any notice. Much to our joy, however, this was one of those extremely rare occasions when a buzz came true. After 2 mad days of queuing in intense cold, we were kitted up, sorted out into chalets and billets, and then sent on 10 days' Christmas leave in our new uniforms. We felt proud on leave though I shudder when I look at the photo that Norman and I had taken together. This is enough about the leave, except to remark that I was full of cold most of the time. Not so tough as I thought!!!

2

TRAINING, BARRACKS AND THE FIRST SEA-GOING SHIP

1941

Back to Skegness for a few days' rifle drill under P O 'Dusty' Miller, surely the maddest, most blasphemous, and yet most efficient gunnery instructor in the Royal Navy.

After that, class 26, split up into two parts, began its course of Signals which was to last for 16 weeks. A London chap shared in the chalet with Norman and I during our course and we made a happy trio, both at work and play. I found the course most interesting and I managed to keep on top of the class most of the time at Morse. In Semaphore and the more intricate knowledge installed in various Signal books, I was not quite so confident and smart.

Whilst ashore on Saturday afternoon we had our first real thrill. On departing from the YMCA, Norman remarked that something was dropping from a single aircraft overhead. We looked, dropped in the snow, and heard a series of thuds nearby. Yes, it was our first *close* taste of bombs. The next street was in a bad way, and a Cinema had been hit. Fortunately the casualties were few.

On several occasions after this, single raiders caused damage and casualties both in Skegness and also in *Royal Arthur*. We had a narrow escape when a piece of shrapnel found its way through our chalet roof, but we were elsewhere at the time. Altogether the camp had rather a rough time as it was never meant to withstand bombs.

On the more cheerful side, we had several long week-ends on one of which I was able to be present at sister Eileen's wedding. Norman and I, the 'Haver & Lee' of the camp as we were called, gave two turns at impromptu concerts in Princes Hall, for which we were rewarded with second prize.

Had it not been for the cold, our stay would have been much more enjoyable. Our part in the invasion scare was to be a part of cyclist platoon. Our duty in case of nearby invasion would be to proceed with bikes and rifles, looking for trouble. No wonder Hitler's boys never came!!!!

Eventually our course and exams finished, in which Norman and I got recommends (the others were half-wits). Fudge, our chalet pal, was drafted to Chatham, whereas Norman and I volunteered to go to Devonport in our ignorance.

We left Skegness just as the nicer weather was appearing, and arrived in Plymouth during the first of five nights of hell let loose. After a long wait in the station, lorries transported us to our second ship, HMS *Drake*, which was fighting a big fire when we got there. The Chief and Petty Officers' mess had received a direct hit, and there were over 200 casualties. The barrack routine had been greatly upset, and we were told our seven-day leave was impossible whilst the large civilian exodus from the city was in force. So Norman and I wandered around the town amidst misery and desolation, and large casualty lists. This went on for three nights and we both wondered if we were to come out alive. Every evening saw civilians, young and old, seeking transport out of the city even if only to sleep in a field or church hall (as we did on more than one occasion). I had wet eyes more than once, believe me. To cut a long and unhappy story short, there were two more big blitzes the following week, making five in all, and we were then allowed to travel for our first seven days' leave, and good night's sleep. How irritated I was in Leeds, to hear more than one person grumbling because the sirens had been going regularly and interrupting sleep. LITTLE DID THEY KNOW HOW FORTUNATE THEY WERE.

It was early May when Norman and I returned to the Valley of Desolation, after missing our train from Leeds, which contained our kit. Kath and Syd were waving the train out, with us standing behind them. Although we arrived back many hours late there were no repercussions, as the barracks were still in a state of chaos.

The next three weeks were spent in various ways, including repairing the Signal School in barracks and building NISSEN huts near Dartmoor prison. We were allowed to talk to the warders and good conduct convicts as they walked through the field in which we were working. I was proud to meet two convicts and one warder from Leeds!!!

Eventually, towards the end of May, Norman and I were drafted to our respective ships, *Black Swan* and *Londonderry*, as Ordinary Signalmen. So we said a fond farewell and henceforth I am on my own. I was to report to Londonderry[1] in the hope of picking up my

---

1   This refers to the city of Londonderry, not the ship of the same name.

ship. As the train from Larne made its way into Derry I could see various classes of men-o-war in the harbour, and I wondered if my sloop was amongst them. Ashore I was told she had left for a foreign commission five days previously, so this was one of my first disappointments at naval organisation. It made things worse when I heard glowing reports of this local ship. So I went onboard the depot ship HMS *Sandhurst* for three more, weary weeks.

Then, along with two others drafted to HMS *Londonderry*, I was given short notice to pack and board an ex-American destroyer, HMS *Sherwood*, to take passage to Newfoundland in the hope of catching up the ship. A quick letter home and our draft went onboard the *Sherwood*.

I reported to the Yeoman on arrival about 8 pm or 2000 Navy time, and was told I would work my passage as a day man from 0800 until 1600. So I found my way to the mess-deck hoping for a good night's sleep, but this was one of many disappointments on the *Sherwood*. The already overcrowded ship's company did not take too kindly to passengers, and the mess-deck was filthy, thick and unfriendly. I did, however, manage to get a bunk, which was more than the other passengers did.

Next morning, my first at sea, saw me reporting on the bridge for duty. It was very rough and we were helping to escort a large convoy. Ahead of us were two famous battleships, *Ramillies* and *Repulse* (later sunk by the Japs). In training I was proud of my ability to read Morse well, but I soon realised twinkling lights in a rough sea were a different proposition.

COMMENTARY

As can be seen from those first two chapters, Dad joined up in Leeds in December 1940 when he was 19 years old. His Certificate of Service shows that he volunteered on 17th December, and the period volunteered for was 'until end of present emergency'.

Norman Brooks, who joined up on the same day, was Dad's best friend before the war and they remained such after the war. When Dad married in 1946, Norman was his best man. He became a newspaper journalist, working on the *Yorkshire Evening News* in Leeds and then later the *Manchester Evening News*. He lived in Sale in Cheshire with his wife Sheila and they had two children.

We used to drive over to see them as a family and vice versa – and that was in the days before the M62, so it was a lengthy and, at times, hairy journey over the Pennines, on winding roads, often shrouded in cloud or fog.

As mentioned earlier, Eileen was Dad's older sister. She married on Easter Saturday, 12th April 1941, at Blenheim Baptist Church, Leeds, with the

Certificate of Service of John Dawson showing he volunteered
"until end of present emergency".

reception at the Mansion Hotel, Roundhay Park, Leeds. Dad was able to be there, as shown in the photograph. Her husband, John Sharkey, had a job in Northern Ireland, and they moved over there after marriage to live in Belfast, first at 43 Pommern Parade, Castlereagh, and then at 267 Castlereagh Road. Hence, Dad's letters to Eileen were sent there, and I think at times she felt as isolated from the family in Leeds as Dad did serving in the Navy.

The Wedding of John's sister, Eileen, to John Sharkey at Blenheim Baptist Church, Leeds and at the Mansion Hotel, Roundhay Park, Leeds on Easter Saturday, 12th April 1941.
Front left is Eileen and John's father and on the right is John, in uniform, with their mother.

Sydney (Syd) was the oldest of the three Dawson children. He had married Kathleen (Kath). He was in the family brush-manufacturing business with his father and his uncle Harold Dawson. Dad had been there with them before the war and returned to become a Partner and then a Director after the war.

THE WAR
By the time Dad joined up, the war had not gone well for Britain or our Allies. Following the so-called Phoney War, which had lasted from October 1939 to May 1940, the Germans started to attack the whole of Western Europe. Holland and Belgium were attacked, followed by France. The British Army was retreating and eventually had to be rescued from the beaches of Dunkirk, where over a period of nine days 330,000 troops were rescued and brought back to Britain. It was not long before France fell to the Germans. German

troops entered Paris on 14th June 1940, soon followed by Adolf Hitler himself. The Germans forced the French to sign an armistice convention and this came into force on 25th June 1940. France was effectively split into two: the German-occupied north and Vichy France in the south.

A particular issue was that although France herself had surrendered, the future of her naval fleet – which was still at liberty – remained a critical question. The fear was that, if captured by the Germans, the ships could be used to bolster their fleet. The British had no intention of allowing this to happen, despite apparent French guarantees, and so the Royal Navy attacked the Vichy fleet.

Clearly the next target for Hitler was Britain. On 1st August 1940, Hitler decreed the Battle of Britain with the command, 'The German air force is to overcome the British air force with all means at its disposal and as soon as possible.' On 13th August the Luftwaffe launched its air offensive against Britain with 1485 sorties. In the most intense attack of the whole Battle of Britain, on 15th August, the Luftwaffe sent a total of 1790 sorties over England. They lost 75 aircraft that day, whilst Britain lost 34. On 3rd September Britain ceded to the USA bases in the West Indies and elsewhere in exchange for 50 destroyers, including HMS *Sherwood*. On 7th September some 300 German bombers escorted by 600 fighters headed for the British capital and bombed London's dockland. On 15th September the RAF claimed to have shot down 183 German aircraft during daylight raids on Britain, a figure which was perhaps exaggerated. Nevertheless, on 17th September, Hitler postponed Operation Sea Lion 'until further notice'. On 12th October he postponed his invasion of Britain until 1941.

However, there was another threat to the security of Britain, which was on the sea. There were severe shipping losses as a result of attacks by surface raiders as well as U-boats of the German Navy.

Britain began to hit back with raids by Bomber Command across Europe. Then in the Western Desert of Africa, between December 1940 and February 1941, the British, in a short but memorable campaign, defeated the Italians in Egypt, Libya and Cyrenaica. It was Britain's first victory on land.

Another aspect of the war, between September 1940 and March 1941 in particular, was the naval war in the Mediterranean. Britain's bases in the Middle East depended on the free passage of Mediterranean convoys, and so the Axis powers resolved to cut off the convoy route from Gibraltar to Alexandria. However, the Royal Navy and the Fleet Air Arm at Taranto and Genoa shattered all Italian hopes of dominating the Mediterranean.

So this was the context of the time at which Dad joined up and played his small part in the Royal Navy and their contribution to the war effort.

THE LETTERS

As mentioned earlier, Dad wrote home both to family in Leeds and to his sister Eileen in Northern Ireland on a regular basis. I have some of these letters, duly cut by the censor, to his sister Eileen and her husband John. I have one or two letters to the family in Leeds.

As has been mentioned in the first two chapters of his Diary, Dad moved down to HMS *Drake*, the naval barracks at Devonport, at a time when that part of Britain was facing terrible air raids on a daily basis. I have a letter which he wrote to Eileen and John on Friday at 8.30 pm which is in an envelope with a postmark dated 25th May 1941 from Plymouth.

Ord.Sig.John R Dawson
JX232329 GI Mess
Grenville Block
HMS Drake Royal Naval Barracks
Devonport

Friday 8.30pm.

Dear Eileen and John

I hope you are both keeping well and getting used to the life in your new surroundings. I have been here now for 3 weeks but as Signals are going out fairly regularly our turn should come in time. Norman (Brooks) has just returned from 5 days on a trawler, which he has quite enjoyed but he prefers a larger ship. Ted and I had a good job this week. [*Section cut out by the censor.*] The weather has been lovely all week. I am a Signal school messenger and fire-watcher tonight, but I have not to report again until 10pm. We also have had Dock yard fire watching one night and that was not too good.

Ted, Jimmy (both from Skegness) and myself have spent our 2 shore leaves this week at Plympton, which is a few miles outside Plymouth. I have slept out both times, though I am only a kid I decided to take the risk. We slept in a rest centre occupied chiefly by bombed out civilians who go out there every night. It was not terribly comfortable, but we had a good sleep, which is our main reason for staying out. We come [*sic*] back at 6.30 am on a lorry. Jimmy and I paid our first visit to a Cinema last night before going to Plympton, and saw 'Date with Destiny' at the Plymouth Odeon. We did not find the place until 7pm so we only saw one picture. [*The next part is cut out by the censor, being on the back of the section on the first page.*] We are probably going on a hike to Tavistock again tomorrow. We went on Sunday and got lifts both ways. As Ted,

Norman and I are different religions we went to the C.of E. service at night but I was not too keen about the service.

(The next section is also edited by the Censor.)

I suppose you have heard how we missed our Bristol train last week and also the Plymouth train from Bristol. It was quite a business and we were 3 hours late but nothing was said. We came down most of the way in a parcel train and were frozen stiff.

I am quite used to the life here now though we will be glad to get out of it. Norman was lucky to get a little experience at sea along with 5 others. We don't do any Signals here but we have to make the best of our odd jobs. I am afraid pyjamas are a luxury now or shall I say a waste of time as we generally only get half undressed when aboard owing to raids and when ashore of course jacket and boots only come off.

I am going to send a little washing home tomorrow as drying seems an impossibility here. (Another small section cut out by the Censor) and in any case it is not safe to leave things about here. Norman and Ted (the Armley lad) both send their best wishes along with mine, and they also hope you are settling down.

I have not heard from home since I returned (except for parcel with no letter), so I don't know what has gone wrong. Fudge also has not written in reply to our letter, so I think he must have got an early draft. I hear that the Skegness lads who went to Chatham have gone on foreign service, but I don't know what will happen to us yet. I know one lad who had to report to Belfast so you never know? Anyway we all have to keep smiling and live a day at a time. Well I will close now with lots of love to you both (don't blush John S) and see you soon (I hope) John R.

The next letter is to the family in Leeds from the same place, on a Tuesday at 7.30 pm:

Ord. Sig. John R. Dawson
JX232329, G1 Mess
HMS Drake Royal Naval Barracks
Devonport

Dear All

Well another week is well on its way and we are still here. Signals are going out and coming in every day, and our turn from draft should come within a fortnight. Ted and I are painters now and our hours are 9–12.30 in the morning and 2.30–4.30 in the afternoon. The job is not so bad and we are allowed to smoke, the only trouble being 2 other lads let us find all the tackle and then they expect to do the painting. We keep giving them the hint to scram, but they have not taken the hint yet.

    I have not got a duty tonight, but Norman and Jimmy have the messenger-fire watching job so for once I have touched lucky. I have just written to Auntie Maude in reply to her nice letter. Miss Hampton has also written a nice letter which I will have to acknowledge this week sometime. I have not heard from Eileen yet but I am still hoping. It is a pity that a few letters have gone astray. Skegness used to make us grumble though in comparison to this everything there seemed almost too good to be true. I bet it is grand there now that warmer weather has arrived.

    Norman, Jimmy and I went to see 'Seven Sinners' at the Odeon last night and I enjoyed it. Jimmy went on to Plympton for the night but the 2 of us risked a night in barracks. There was only one disturbance, but we put our trousers on and went to sleep again, thereby having a good nights sleep. I feel tired again tonight so I will be going early to bed again.

    NAAFI seems to be getting more food in these days and as a result we are all spending quite a lot on tea and buns to satisfy our appetites. We will have to cut it down or else our pockets will be empty. Pay day is on Thursday so we have something to look forward to.

    I was looking at last week's 'Illustrated' in which there were several pages about Plymouth. If Daddy saw it it would enlighten him a lot more than I can about the great work being done in a certain village (Plympton of course). I was rather surprised to see the village in question mentioned once by name.

    We found a YMCA and Joe H open in Plymouth last night although all around was destruction. It is marvellous how several buildings manage to go unscratched in a district which is nothing but rubble apart from them. Incidentally the food at the YMCA was okay.

I had a shower bath tonight and cleaned myself up a bit, though the water was cold. I will be glad when I can manage a good hot bath.

I am sorry Mr Knight's services have not been obtained (Miss Hampton told me) and I expect that means more work for Daddy. She also said that Mother looked very well and I hope that goes for you all. I do not know when Daddy gives his speech but I wish him the best of luck.[2]

Weekend leave seems to have been stopped for good here, so our chance of a trip to Torquay or somewhere is off. It is a pity as it would be grand to get away for a couple of days. I have written my usual 4 sides now so I will close by sending all my love and God bless you all, John.

There is a further letter to Eileen and John, again undated other than saying 'Saturday 8pm 1941' but I think it was about the same time (late May 1941) and it reads as follows:

> G1 Mess
> Grenville Block
> Royal Naval Barracks
> Devonport
> Plymouth

Dear Eileen and John

I hope you are both well and settling down better. I have not heard from you yet so I do not know if my other letter arrived. We are still here and likely to be for a week or two as Ted, Norman and myself are in the Princetown working party on a special job. We are taking all our baggage etc on Monday as we are going to stay there day and night. I never thought that I would see convicts every day as we do on our new job. Entertainment there will probably be poor, but the food is good and there is more of it than in the barracks. Up to now we have been going there and back in lorries every day arriving in barracks about 6pm. We have seen two good pictures this week 'Seven Sinners' and 'Road to Frisco.'

Before I got on this Princetown job I had been covering broken window panes and painting rooms in a damaged barracks building. We seem, in fact, to do all sorts of jobs excepting the one we joined up for. Still we do not grumble a lot as it does not help. To see the

---
2   I am not sure what any of this is about other than to do with Church.

Plymouth people having to go out every night in lorries and sleep on hard floors makes us realise that others are worse off than us by a long way. Their spirit, however, is wonderful as we have found when we have gone out to surrounding districts on our nights ashore.

Jimmy, our other pal, went yesterday for a week on a Polish craft. Our new job has spoilt my chance of a week in a trawler etc but it should not interfere with our drafting when our turn comes, which I hope will not be too long.

I have received 2 parcels from Leeds, one from home and one from Brethericks. One or two letters have not arrived though. I hope you are receiving the letters from home and I expect you look forward to them as I do.

I have managed to get a hot shower tonight which is something quite novel here. I sent some washing home last Monday as drying is a big problem here and it has come back safely. We have had a fair share of rain in these last few days, after a lovely warm spell which was grand after Butlins.

One of the chaps working with us is a Leeds chap and he was very friendly with Noel Scottern. He has a photo of the football team he used to play in and Noel is on it. Also one of the Warders we have spoken to at Dartmoor used to live barely a hundred yards from Ted. A small world.

I have had nice letters from Miss Hampton and Auntie Maude and both mentioned you in very favourable terms wishing you happiness in your new sphere.

I have nothing else much to say except that I often think of you and I hope the day will hasten when we can all meet again.

Cheerio for now and all the best, Brother John.

There is then a letter sent when he was in Londonderry:

Ord. Sig. John R Dawson
11 Mess JX232329
HMS Sandhurst
c/o GPO London

Mon 5.45pm

Dear Eileen

Thank you very much indeed for your very nice letter which I received yesterday just before going ashore. From the tone of your letter

I think you are probably thinking I have not made much of an effort to come and see you. I can honestly say that nothing would suit me better than to able to come across you both again. As you say there are difficulties and I am afraid that until I get on my own ship it will be impossible for me to come to you. The only possible chance now would be a Saturday or Sunday, and then everything would have to be done on chance. Would I get a train in good time, how long to find you and would you be in and would I be certain to get back aboard by 11pm? (Incidentally we do not go ashore until 1.15pm). You see, we can get no 'concessions' until we are aboard our own ship.

You said you could come here at a moment's notice. Well if that is so is there any possible chance of you both coming on Saturday next June 21st? Naturally you will not have time to get a letter back by then (yours took a long time didn't it), but I will make arrangements just hoping. You will have to remember that if our ship comes everything might go wrong, but on the other hand even if she does she might be in a few days. So you see it will only be on chance if you do come and you would have to be prepared to have a day out on your own if things went wrong. I am afraid I am putting everything onto you but I really am keen to see you and while there is a chance it would be a shame to miss it.

Anyway shall we say 1.45pm–2pm somewhere on the Bridge or if not then, 4.30–5pm same place. I certainly am asking a lot but it has given me something to write about and if by any chance you could trouble to come, my opportunity to return the visit ought to come in the future with more time to do it.

Well Jock and I had quite a nice afternoon and evening ashore yesterday. A walk and seat in the park, tea, the Presbyterian Church and then a couple of hours or so with two young ladies. We saw one of them in the Choir and then met her with a friend later on the main street. It was not so bad but I was not too struck and although we have made the date for tomorrow I'm afraid I may not turn up. First looks were good but conversation can change opinions.

Suppertime so lots of love and keep smiling. I would love to see you so let's hope, love from John

COMMENTARY

As we saw in Chapter 2 of the Diary, Dad was given short notice to board HMS *Sherwood* and so the planned meeting could not take place and he wrote a further letter a day or two later to his sister as follows:

Wed 6.30pm

Dear Eileen

Do not come Saturday as we are under sail soon in a vessel in order to catch our ship. If you do not hear from me for a while do not worry. I will do my best. The testing time has now come and I will have to do my best.

Lots of love John

COMMENTARY
That letter was in an envelope with the postmark 'Londonderry 6am 19th June 1941', two days before the planned meeting.

3

DISILLUSIONMENT AND THE TOUGHENING UP PROCESS

THE DIARY (CONTINUED)
An hour or two on the bridge and I had a feeling that my worst hopes were soon to be realised. I felt bad, and I must have looked even worse, as the Officer of the Watch asked me if it were my first trip. I replied in the affirmative, but bravely said that I would be quite OK. Imagine my embarrassment when, half an hour later, 'I brought my heart up' all over the place. The OOW and Yeoman were very decent and I was told to rest on the upper deck until I felt better. This I did, feeling utterly despondent.

At dinner time I struggled to the mess in an endeavour to eat and conquer, but what went down soon came up. So the rest of my first day at sea was spent miserably praying for a torpedo to come and end it all. What a day, and I wondered if it would always be the same!!!

Next day I awoke with trepidation, and found it was too rough to get aft for a wash. (The water was only on for two 10-minute spells each day, and if too rough one just had to do without.) Much to my joy, however, I got through the day without being sick, and I was able to give the signal staff what little help I could.

After a few similar days we had to leave the convoy and call at Hval Fjord, Iceland with engine trouble. I was informed that this was a regular thing with the 50 ex-American lend-lease destroyers. The *Sherwood* soon left, but there was a recurrence of the trouble whilst investigating a submarine contact at high-speed, and we once again returned. It was then decided to transfer the passengers to HMCS *Ottawa* which was shortly to escort a convoy to St John's, Newfoundland.

I was not in the least sorry to leave the dirty, unfriendly *Sherwood* and even on my last day onboard, the leading seaman of our mess tried to 'pinch' my oilskin. By this time, however, I was not quite so green, and I told him what I thought of the ship in general and himself in particular. So I had a tough breaking-in process on my first sea-going ship.

4

HMCS *OTTAWA*

The month of June 1941 was well under way when we rode a whaler over to the Canadian Captain 'D' in Hval Fjord. I was soon shown into the watchkeepers' mess, comprising signalmen, telegraphists and quartermasters. What a difference. The mess was clean, and everyone seemed eager to make an Englishman feel at home. The Chief Yeoman told all the Signal staff that I was fresh out of training, and that I was to be given every help during the 10-day convoy trip.

Before leaving Iceland the ship moved to the port of Reykjavik, where I was able to have a run ashore with the other two chaps on draft with me, one a steward, the other a torpedoman. I found the place clean, the girls very attractive, the shops well-stocked, but a decided coldness on the part of the civilians. In June, of course, there were 24 hours of light each day, and it was a well-known fact that local girls were afraid to 'fraternise', for what their elders would say or do to them.

To cut a long and interesting story short, the *Ottawa* eventually sailed in sole charge of a large convoy and escort, at the slow speed of 9 knots. I was given every opportunity to transmit and read signals, besides the main duty of an Ordinary Sig., i.e. in writing down and acting as general handyman for senior ratings. I became quite friendly with all the staff, and I had to adapt myself to coffee in preference to tea. A joke in the mess was my Yorkshire habit of asking for treacle instead of golden syrup.

I was sick a couple of times, but there were plenty of hardened sailors who shared the doubtful pleasure, so I was not dismayed.

After an interesting 10 days, and uneventful as far as the enemy was concerned, we entered St John's harbour, Newfoundland. There was no sign of the elusive HMS *Londonderry*, so the three of us were sent over to the large base ship, HMS *Forth*. I was sorry to leave such a happy ship manned by such friendly Canadians.

COMMENTARY

Unfortunately, as mentioned in the section on The Ships, the *Ottawa* was sunk on 14th September 1942. She was hit by two torpedoes from a German U-boat while escorting a convoy. One hundred and fourteen crew were lost with 65 survivors.

THE LETTERS (CONTINUED)

2/7/41
HMS Ottawa

Dear Eileen and John

Hope you received my last letter and I am only too sorry that I have so little to tell you. Since I wrote I have changed ships as the first one, after one or two incidents, has had its destination changed. My present ship is much better in every way and for once I am able to keep everything reasonably clean. The crew seem OK and are very helpful, though I am pretty raw in comparison.

I am separated from Wally and Jock so I am having to stand on my own feet more than ever now. We are still in harbour at the previous spot I vaguely mentioned, and I will be glad as I think everyone aboard will be when we get on our way.

I will be glad when I receive any letters either from you or home as I certainly miss them, but naturally all this hopping about makes it very difficult. Still it is all part of Navy life and one has to keep a lot of trust in faith and hope. To think that I used to get letters or parcels almost every day. Certainly different at sea.

It will soon be water time now so, as I want to do some more washing I will finish this measly letter. I seem to get worse every time I write, as I have so little to say, but the main thing is to constantly to keep you aware of my existence. (That sounds good) hope you are both well and are really settled down

Your loving brother John

5

HMS *FORTH* - JULY 1941–1943

THE DIARY (CONTINUED)

PART 1 – IN ST JOHN'S, NEWFOUNDLAND AND A TRIP TO THE USA

I realise that my first six months or so in the Navy has taken a lot of space, but I do not apologise. I have emphasised those first few months in order to prove that I had to learn the hard way. I had not been allowed to settle down to one ship or one crowd of chaps, and for the first time in my life I was truly dependent on myself, even though the three of us were in the 'same boat'. On duty, however, I was definitely on my own.

My introduction to the *Forth* was not an attractive one, as I found myself helping to scrub the flag deck, almost as soon as I had found my billet. I was able to go ashore into St John's with the torpedoman previously mentioned, and we lived on the fat of the land. There was plenty of everything in the way of fruit, sweets and food generally. I found ice-cream and apple pie to be my favourite dish.

The living conditions for civilians were rather primitive, and most of the buildings were mainly of wooden structure. The cinemas were not too bad, but one was not allowed to smoke, a rule which was also enforced in Canada and America, chiefly due to the inadequate ventilation in hot weather. It was whilst at St John's that I was able to see 'Gone With The Wind', and I was surprised to find that I enjoyed it.

Back to the *Forth*. She was a two-funnelled depot ship, quite modern, originally built as a submarine parent ship but at St John's was carrying out the duties as nerve centre for all men-o-war engaged on Atlantic convoy work.

My first few weeks were spent on the flag deck along with other 'pool' ratings. A 'pool' rating is one who lives and works on a base ship, whilst awaiting draft to another ship. I did quite well at signal exercises, and the Signal Boatswain, Mr Caplan, began to take an interest

John Dawson after joining his first ship HMS *Forth*.

in my welfare. I know for a fact that he stopped two sea-going drafts for me, and the draft to HMS *Londonderry* was a thing of the past. Eventually he asked me if I would like to stay onboard as ship's company. I answered that I was not keen, as I was keen to go to sea. He told me, in confidence, that the *Forth* would soon be leaving St John's and going to Scotland via America. This sounded good and I agreed to stay onboard. I was soon sent into the SDO (Signal Distributing Office), which contained a mass of telephones, typewriters and signals.

Here I had to work like a Trojan for several weeks, chiefly as telephonist, and I was never happy. I complained to Mr Caplan that I detested office work and wanted to be doing visual work. He said the office work was all part of a good signalman's groundwork, and I appreciated it later, if not then. He said I would return to the flag deck when I became a Signalman.

Needless to say my spare time was then concentrated on swotting up, and I was very proud when I passed for signalman on September 1st with flying colours, and 1/3 a day more. I then became a visual worker again and a few days later the *Forth* prepared to sail. Mr Caplan stayed behind on the relief depot ship, but although he was not popular generally, I found him a great help during my short association.

My job for leaving harbour was to stand by the ensign, and I felt very proud as we left St John's with a large, waving crowd to see us off. The Captain nearly hit the boom on the way out, but a miss is as good as a mile.

The next 10 days was spent visiting certain American ports to leave torpedoes for our submarines. (Incidentally this was when the USA was neutral!!!)

We paid quick calls to Newport, New Portsmouth, Boston before arriving at New London, where we were to put in for 4 days. Our visit caused quite a sensation, and invitations were soon received for parties to be entertained ashore. I had two 'nights out'. On the first, two busloads of us had a 160-mile trip to New York, where we arrived at 6 pm and left at 6 am the following morning. Highlights of that great night for me were, a) Broadway and the traffic, b) the Automat cafes, c) free seats at a Joe E. Brown broadcast in Radio City, d) the Rainbow Room and the view from the top of Radio City, and e) the Aid to Britain ball at which we were guests of honour, WHAT AN EXPERIENCE!!!

My other day out was in New London, when 50 of us were guests of local inhabitants. A football match and tea were the main attractions arranged for us.

All good things come to an end, and the ship had to leave for the port of Halifax, Canada. We found this port a hive of activity, and several troopships were already assembling for our convoy. I had one run ashore in Halifax with two other signalmen, but was not able to form much of an impression. The following day all was ready for the trip *home*.

PART 2 – AN UNEVENTFUL CONVOY, HOME AND OUR NEW JOB

It was a 17-knot convoy designed to beat the U-boat, and our 8-day trip was enjoyable, busy and uneventful except that one ship could not maintain the speed and had to be left behind. There was no place for a straggler. I noticed the *Ottawa* amongst the escort.

A slow convoy which left after us was attacked twice on the homeward journey, and suffered rather bad losses. We were lucky to be in a fast moving convoy.

We left the majority of the convoy off Scotland, and proceeded up the Clyde to Greenock. It was at Greenock that I collected my mail for the 3 months I had been away from *Drake*. I received 61 letters altogether!!! Incidentally this trip had given me my first taste of night-watches at sea, especially the dreaded Middle (midnight to 4 am). One amusing incident on the trip is worth mentioning. Our Captain ordered a depth charge to be dropped for exercise, but the wrong indicator was pressed and a lifebuoy was seen harmlessly floating away!!!

After 24 hours at Greenock we had a destroyer escort to take us round the north of Scotland to our next port of call, Rosyth, where the ship was to undergo a refit. As soon as we passed under the famous Forth bridge our Captain applied for 14 days' leave each watch, and I was in the first batch.

Although my life had not yet been full of excitement, I found plenty to talk about in good old Leeds. This was in mid-November 1941.

On my return from leave I found the ship was in dry dock, and conditions were therefore anything but good. Four of us in our branch went to the Dockyard Signal Station every morning for instructions, with a view to higher rating. Being fairly new as a Signalman I was not confident of passing for TO (trained operator), but I had nothing to lose. Anyhow we all passed our respective exams, so that was another 2d a day for me.

We were in Rosyth over Christmas 1941, and we managed to have enjoyable runs ashore in Rosyth, Dunfermline and Edinburgh. My particular pals in those days were Higgy and Buck Taylor. I was with Buck for almost 15 months after this, but Higgy was drafted and later was seriously injured whilst on Russian convoy work onboard a Polish destroyer.

Whilst undergoing the refit my job as a TO was leading hand of a watch in the SDO, but there was not much work. Towards the end of the refit we were all employed on generally straightening up the flag deck, flag lockers, halyards, and lamps etc., prior to proceeding to the Holy Loch, Dunoon, where we were due in mid-January 1942 for work as submarine parent ship.

The *Forth* left Rosyth basin for a buoy one early morning, and I was sent away with Aldis lamp and battery in the motor boat to point out the correct one. The job was done correctly, but whilst clambering inboard the Aldis shoulder strap parted and I returned minus one battery. This was my one and only 'rattle-boat' and I became a Commander's defaulter. ('Rattle-boat' is a defaulter, with prospect of punishment.) I think he believed my tale of woe as I was dismissed with a caution.

On arrival at Holy Loch the first 24 hours was a real nightmare. We went alongside the *Titania* whom we were to relieve, and there was quite a delay in transferring the telephone and teleprinter cables from her to us. Whilst this was going on, signals by lamp were coming in from all sides, from escort vessels, submarines and the shore signal station. My 'opposite number' on watch was not a good Morse reader, so I had very little rest in that first 24 hours. *Titania* left the following day and we became the boss.

Our new work briefly was this. We were responsible for the working up programmes of all new submarines, and also the base for submarines on patrol in the Atlantic and North Sea. The ship's staff were responsible for repair and maintenance, the torpedoes were supplied from us, and the staff officers and communication branches were responsible for the sailing and safety of all submarines working under our orders. By teleprinter we were in touch with all naval stations throughout the British Isles, and any urgent signals to subs on patrol were passed from us to Whitehall W/T[3] for transmission to the respective addressees, who received but did not answer.

THE LETTERS (CONTINUED)

Dad wrote a few letters from HMS *Forth* during this period and some of these are set out below. The first one is dated 26th July 1941:

---

3 Wireless telegraphy.

John Dawson

> Ord. Sig. J. Dawson
> JX232329
> 35 Mess
> HMS Forth
> c/o GPO London

Dear Eileen

Just a few lines to let you know I am still going strong. My original draft has now been cancelled and I am staying here for a while undergoing instruction. I do not mind a lot really, but my one big worry is that Wally and I are now in different watches and cannot go ashore together. As Jock does not go ashore (in any case he is in the other watch), I will have the unusual experience of going on my own tomorrow. Quite a change after a long friendship with Norman and others since leaving home.

I have put my address on as I may be here a while, although on the other hand I may not. Anyway if I don't get settled so I can receive letters, I will have to write to myself. I hear that England is having a grand summer so far, and I hope you have been lucky in that respect. I often wonder what would have happened to me if I had caught my ship straight away. There are a lot of 'ifs' in life, though; but it makes one wonder just the same.

This is quite a good place for eats ashore though one has to have plenty of money to really make the best of it. Wally and I used to be always getting something to eat when we were ashore together, especially ices and fruit. I have been twice to the pictures. The first title I cannot remember, but the other was 'Flame of New Orleans' with Marlene Dietrich. Not bad but a trifle fantastic.

Lastly I hope you are both well and lots of love and good wishes,

From John

Another letter is dated 3rd August 1941:

Ord. Sig. J. Dawson
51 Mess
HMS Forth
c/o GPO London

Dear Eileen

I cannot remember which day I wrote to you last, but I think it is your turn to hear from me. The weather has not been so good lately and we are having plenty of rain. Smithy (my new shore mate) and myself got wet through yesterday as we went without coats. We went to see 'Gone With the Wind' at night, and I certainly enjoyed it, although I have a job to keep awake at the pictures these days. It was mid-night before it finished. We went to the pictures on all three leaves last week, and the first time I slept through most of the programme.

Jock and Wally are in different watches to me so I cannot go with them, though Jock never goes anyway.

Two of the lads who had travelled about for so long with us, have now rejoined their ship and were they glad? They were different to us as they had been on the ship earlier but missed it owing to both being ill ashore in hospital.

I have done quite a lot of letter writing lately and it is quite a job to send and not receive, as I soon run out of news. Life is not bad here but it would be a lot better if there was chance of a little leave. I have no idea when I will see home again, and as things have turned out it's a good job I managed to get home quite a lot while training. At any rate I will be away from home for my birthday for the first time. Twenty sounds quite old to me, so I hope it does not come too quickly. Have you had a holiday this summer? If so I hope you had a grand time with some of the good weather which England, at any rate, has been having.

I often wonder how Norman is going on, and when we tried to casually say good bye at Devonport, I don't suppose either of us really thought that our chances of meeting before the end of the war were practically nil. I have seen quite a few lads from different ships I knew from these days, but Norman's ship is not on this run worse luck.

Well my time is up, or shall I say honestly that I cannot conjure up anything more to say. Anyway lots of love and best wishes to you both, from your loving brother,

John.

John Dawson

Another letter is dated 13th August 1941:

> Ord. Sig. J. Dawson
> 51 Mess
> HMS Forth
> c/o GPO London

Dear Eileen

Here's hoping you are well and still occasionally thinking of little Johnnie, the twirp. I am very conscientious this week as tonight will be the fourth night in five I have been duty aboard [*sic*]. I did a watch Saturday, changed watches Sunday and therefore did another, went ashore Monday, duty last night and again tonight and I got permission to change so as to be able to go ashore with Smithy, my new pal.

Wally, who I have often mentioned, is now at sea on a [*cut by censor*] as a temporary member of the crew. He was not too pleased as he does not like life at sea at all. I am sorry for him as he is a really good chap, and he has been pretty decent to me for the length of our short friendship. (That phrase does not read well but as usual the idea's there).

I have been on here a month now and time has certainly gone quickly. The hours are pretty long but I have been interested and that has helped a lot. The night watches often drag terribly, especially the middle, and it is a job keeping awake when there is nothing doing. I much prefer a watch when there is a little activity, as it not only passes time quicker but it gives one more experience at the job.

I hope you are both well and I still looking forward [*sic*] to my first mail. Lack of news from home is the worst part of being over here, but there are fellows worse off than me in other ways so I must not grumble. Supper time now so cheerio for now and lots of love,

From brother John.

Those last letters were written from 51 Mess and the next is from 33 Mess as is explained in the letter itself.

Dated 23rd August 1941:

Ord. Sig. J. Dawson
33 Mess
HMS Forth
c/o GPO London

Dear Eileen

As you will see my Mess has changed, or least it will be doing any day now. I have now been 'promoted' to Ship's company much against my will as it necessitates me going into the office. I had my first spell there this morning and I did not enjoy it very much. Still it is essential for a Signalman to have an all-round training so I will reap the benefit in the future, I suppose. The hours I have now will not give me as much spare time to study the practical side, but such is life.

I have not been ashore since Tuesday so I am going tonight. Unluckily all my pals are in a different watch and that is why I have not bothered much lately. That is the worst part of this life, as one never seems to be able to get really settled down for much of a spell to a definite routine.

I hope you are both well and I often look at the wedding photo I still have in my possession. Certainly that was a really big occasion and I include that as one of my happiest memories. Now I am staying on here, my big hope is that the ship may make a move homeward, but one cannot do more than speculate about that.

I have regretted not sending a cable home when I first arrived here, as the delay is making me impatient. I have received no mail yet but eventually it should arrive.

Whatever the future may bring, without any boasting at all, I have done my best and certainly I have learnt a lot on here. Both the Signal bosun and Yeoman have quietly praised me, and told me to keep it up. That is chiefly why I am now a permanent part of the ship's company. I am afraid I will not be as good in the office but I will do my best.

Not much else to say except to send all my love, and best wishes for the future,

Your loving brother,

John.

Each of those letters so far in this section were clearly written in Newfoundland. There is a gap of nearly two months before the next letter, which was also sent from there but which refers to the trip to the United States. The letter is dated 8th October 1941:

Sig. J. R. Dawson
33 Mess
HMS Forth
c/o GPO London

Dear Eileen

Thanks a lot for your letter dated 19/8 which I received a fortnight ago, but did not reply to at once as it would not have arrived any sooner. No, I have not been all over the world yet, but since last writing the ship has visited 2 other countries making five since I left England. From one of the places we visited, the crew received permission to run two coaches (roughly 60 men), for a day's outing to what must be the world's gayest city. It was a marvellous trip and well worth the week's pay which it cost to get there alone. We all came back broke or almost so, and the week we have been in our present port, hardly anyone has been ashore. I have been once, but it seemed rather weak after the great time we had in the [*cut by censor*] I expect you were quite thrilled to travel with a film star, but you can't have it all your own way you know. The four of us who stuck together on the previously mentioned trip, managed to 'wangle' tickets for a broadcast which included a certain Joe E. Brown. I have numerous memories of that day which I will have to keep in my mind for the right occasion.

 I was glad to hear everyone at your end is well, as naturally lack of news always tends to make one worry a little. I hope you are very happy and proud in your new home which I would love to see. I was also very pleased to hear that you managed to get to England for a week.

 As I look at today's date I realise that time is passing quickly, and you are probably having very cold weather at this time. It is not too bad here, though one has to keep well wrapped up for night watches. We have to turn out at 05.45 every morning as well so we are certainly not being spoilt. I know if I get home on leave anytime Mother will have a job to get me up in a morning.

 We had a concert on board the other night, the first since I joined the ship, and I had a really good laugh. I have palled up with a Yorkshire lad and he has the most infectious laugh I have ever come across, and when he really gets going he is uncontrollable. He is going with a Leeds girl so I hope we get leave together when the time comes.

Well cheerio for the present, Eileen and give my regards to John won't you? Lots of love from

John.

COMMENTARY
USA'S ISOLATIONISM AND ENTERING INTO WAR
When war broke out in Europe in September 1939, although the great majority of Americans favoured the Allies, they were strongly opposed to joining the struggle against Germany. This conflict of views became harder and harder to manage as France fell and the war went from bad to worse for the Allies in 1940 and 1941.

President Roosevelt wanted to assist the Allies, especially Britain, but to keep in with popular opinion he had to promise not to send American troops to fight in Europe. Thus, he decided that his best course was to seek support for all aid short of war, and this he did during 1941. He continued to face isolationism in Congress and amongst the American people. This was not a new concept but a long-held one in America.

Roosevelt had persuaded Congress to agree a billion and a half dollars in May 1941 – after Germany's offensive in Western Europe – to mechanise the Army and expand aircraft production. Soon after, following Dunkirk, Congress agreed another billion dollars for the Army and nearly seven hundred million dollars for the Navy.

France and Britain pleaded with Roosevelt to enter the war or at least to declare non-belligerency, which was one step better than neutrality. Churchill made a number of specific requests, including the loan of forty or fifty destroyers and that supplies from the USA should continue to Britain even after her financial reserves had been used up.

At this stage, Roosevelt rejected the loan of destroyers and sending supplies without cash payment, the latter being specifically forbidden by the neutrality laws. However, in a speech on 10th June 1940, he attacked Italy and promised material support to the Allies. The following day, Churchill asked again for the loan of destroyers. Unfortunately, at the end of June, Congress agreed a new law forbidding the disposal of any navy or army equipment unless the service chiefs certified them as 'not essential for defense'.

A way round this was found, however. It was agreed to exchange the destroyers for British bases in the Western Hemisphere, which it was argued would strengthen US defence. The deal was well received by the American public. Germany had by now conquered France, the Allies were suffering defeats and Americans began to realise that perhaps even South America could be threatened by the Germans.

Roosevelt decided to stand for a third term as President. His Republican opponent was Wendell Willkie, also an internationalist. Thus, there was bi-partisan support for Roosevelt's foreign policy of aiding the Allies, albeit not joining the conflict. Roosevelt won the election in November 1940 on this basis.

It became ever clearer that only increased US aid could help to save Britain from defeat. This could only be achieved by supplying Britain's needs without payment. Hence lending or leasing war material was the concept developed. Lend-lease was overwhelmingly approved by Congress after lengthy debate. The aim, however, remained to keep America out of the war itself. Thus, Roosevelt would not take the step, for example, to provide US naval support for convoys to Britain.

The Americans also still saw the most direct threat to them as being from Japan. The signing of the Russo-Japanese neutrality pact in April 1941 brought renewed belligerency in Japan's pronouncements on Asian affairs. The US Pacific fleet had to be maintained to deter Japan. However, the German invasion of Russia in June 1941 changed the picture again. Now not only the British but also the Russians were pressing the USA to join in the war. However, the isolationist views in America re-emerged and the House of Representatives only supported by a majority of one the extension of conscription for a further 18 months.

After the invasion of Russia by Germany, Japanese forces were freed up to threaten Southeast Asia. American interests there were threatened alongside British and Dutch interests. Roosevelt began to toughen up his views. From July, preparations were made to occupy Iceland, so freeing up British troops. On 13th November 1941, by narrow majorities, Congress agreed to repeal the Neutrality Act. Hitler, in spite of greater US support for the Allies, refused at this stage to declare war on the USA.

However, events were moving forward in the Far East. Japanese troops invaded French Indo-China. The US froze Japanese funds in America and banned oil exports to Japan. Effectively trade was halted by America together with Britain and the Netherlands. All evidence now showed that the Japanese were preparing for war in Southeast Asia. In October 1941, the Japanese Navy was making its final preparations to attack Pearl Harbor in Hawaii. The Americans presented the Japanese with a peace plan, but this would have meant Japan ending its attacks in Asia and was unacceptable to Japan. On 7th December 1941 Japan attacked Pearl Harbor. On 8th December, Britain, the USA and the Netherlands declared war on Japan, and on 11th December Germany and Italy declared war on the USA.

EUROPE AND THE MEDITERRANEAN

In March and April 1941, Germany attacked and defeated Yugoslavia. Also in March 1941 the British agreed a plan with Greece for the defence of that country. However, in April, Germany invaded Greece. The country was occupied and defeated by the end of the month, with the British evacuating her last forces on 29th April.

In May 1941 the Germans invaded Crete, which British, Commonwealth and Greek troops were defending. It was the greatest airborne troop offensive mounted by the Germans in the war. By the end of May, the British had evacuated and the island was in German hands.

In the Western Desert of North Africa, German troops led by Rommel began to cause setbacks for the Allies from April 1941. On the other hand, in the Middle East, the Allies successfully defeated the Iraqis and the Vichy French in Iraq, Syria and Lebanon over a period from late April to July 1941. It was only in late 1941 and early 1942 that the British started to challenge Rommel's dominance in North Africa. Also between March and June 1941, Malta successfully resisted Italian and German attacks to retain its vital strategic role in the Mediterranean for the Allies.

Meanwhile, the German battleship *Bismarck* broke out into the North Sea. She was intercepted by the Royal Navy, but HMS *Hood* was sunk and *Bismarck* escaped. However, other ships then closed in with support from the Fleet Air Arm and the *Bismarck* was eventually sunk on 27th May 1941.

THE DIARY (CONTINUED)
PART 3 – MY WORK, IMPRESSIONS, AND HOW CONSCIENCE OVERCAME SECURITY

My first job at Holy Loch was to work alternate 24 hours at the shore signal station on Ardnadam Pier. The station contained a small telephone exchange connected to the *Forth* and *Al Rawdah* (an accommodation ship for sub crews), and also the WRNS hostel. There was a confidential telephone to all Naval stations in the British Isles, two teleprinters, signalling gear, a wireless, a stove for cooking, and altogether quite a compact little place.

Another TO and myself originally manned it between us from 7.30 am to 11 pm each day. As long as the communication system onboard the ship was 100% perfect, our job was mainly to arrange for boats to and from the pier and to be ready for any emergency. Wrens worked on the *Forth* all day, but were not allowed onboard at night. So at 10.30 pm each evening one Wren and a signal boatswain or warrant telegraphist came to the shore station for the night. At 11 pm I locked the pier gate and returned to the ship.

The Commander of the *Forth* disliked this idea, of one male and one female being locked away in this hut every night. (After all, the officers were not old, and some of the girls most attractive!!!) So a third party was ordered to sleep there and the fellow TO and myself were detailed off. So we went there alternate days for the full 24 hours, taking our own food and bedding. Normally I would turn in about midnight and be awakened at 6 am with a cup of tea by the duty Wren. HAPPY DAYS!!!!

On more than one occasion the heavy seas dislocated the cables to the ship, in which case our shore station became the nerve centre of the flotilla. Two occasions especially spring to mind. On the first it was too rough for any transport to the ship, so 2 Wrens, the Signal Boatswain and I had 48 hours' work without relief. By this time I had learned to manipulate a teleprinter, and between us we managed to snatch a little sleep in turn. I had to transmit and receive signals by light to and from the *Forth* day and night, so it was hard work. The Boatswain and I had to prepare the meals, as the two girls did not even know how to fry egg and bacon!!

The other occasion was when the cables had to undergo major repairs. So for 10 days, 4 Wrens, 4 Wren Cypher Officers, another signalman and myself had the ship 'on our backs'. There was no room for a male Signal Officer to sleep there as well, so Arthur and I were surrounded by a bevy of beauty (?) during that busy period. I learned quite a lot about the fairer sex during that time!!!

Anyway I had this job for six months, during which I had many runs ashore into Dunoon, and alternate Saturday trips to Glasgow.

Meanwhile onboard the ship four leading signalmen were in four watches in the CCO (Central Communication Office). They were responsible for the receipt, transmission and distribution of all signals to and from the ship and submarines. It was an unenviable job, chock full of responsibility. Each leading signalman had under him one coder, three Wrens, and 2 signalmen on the bridge, plus a messenger.

10 Days' leave were given every six months, so I was told to take over LHOW (leading hand of watch), in the CCO for the leave periods. Another signalman relieved me at the shore station. At first it was a nightmare, as I had only 18 months in the Navy, whereas the others had all been in the service for over 5 years. Anyway I was eager to hold my own, and with the help of Fred Hunt and 'Windy' Gale especially, I kept out of any real trouble. The Wrens were awkward and lazy at times, but they could have been worse. The Boatswain seemed quite pleased at my quick grasp of the job, and even at the termination of the leave he would not take me off the job. So a leading

signalman was made a day man, and I continued watch-keeping for almost 12 months at the same sort of work.

Most of the signal staff were either men with long service whose practical ability was not so brilliant, or else young chaps who were not interested or unable to read Morse or Semaphore at any speed. So I got 'roped' in for several odd, extra jobs. A trawler would go into nearby lochs to exercise with subs, and a signalman would go to maintain communication. I found the fresh air and work most interesting after the monotonous office work.

Meanwhile life was pretty good for me in Dunoon. Originally we had not slept ashore very often as we had not been able to get settled digs. Most landladies would take sailors in during the quiet periods, but not in spring or summer. I was fortunate eventually to be introduced to a Mrs Thompson who said she could put up two of us each night, winter and summer, for very fair prices. As our staff worked 24 hours about on the ship, I picked three reliable chaps to make up a foursome, and two of us slept there alternate nights.

The room consisted of a table, two comfy chairs, a fire, and double bed, and became a home from home for us. Mrs Thompson and her daughter Betty provided us with a meal at night and also in the morning. If, through leave or illness, one of us were unable to go, I would find a suitable substitute so as to keep the ball rolling. At different times my brother, his wife, Mother, Betty and Dad spent holidays in Dunoon and a visit to Mrs Thompson was always on the agenda. When on Saturday shore leave my pals and I would visit Glasgow, where we stayed in a boarding house at Cessnock for 5/- a night. I was able to see two international football matches at Hampden Park along with over 100,000 others, so another life-long ambition was achieved.

Whilst returning to the ship from my 10 days' leave one night, I missed the last ferry, and tried to get across to Holy Loch from Gourock in a motor-boat. The sea was too rough, the engine stopped and the boat began to leak. There were two of us and bailing out was quite an ordeal. As it was dark I soaked a white shirt in oil, lit it, and hopefully waved it on a stick. This brought no signs of rescue, so we collected all the spare oil in a bucket and set fire to that. Eventually the pilot boat came out and we were towed back to Gourock. I had to make a signed statement at the police station, and I returned to the *Forth* next morning, 10 hours late. My story and appearance carried the day and I was not punished. Quite an adventure.

A joke in the Navy is that a depot ship has to go to sea once a year to earn the duty-free cigarettes!!! Be that as it may, but the *Forth* left Holy Loch for one week to go into dock at Glasgow, and to have a few exercises. During that week most of our staff were transferred, with the WRNS, to the relief ship, HMS *Wolfe*. The only remark I have on that week, is that we were all relieved to return to the *Forth*.

Time passed all too quickly, and though I found the work interesting and full of responsibility I realised over and over again that my conscience was troubling me. The Boatswain asked me many times to let him pass me for Leading Sig. (Lower grade), but I realised it would probably mean a sea-going draft and I had been doing office work for 18 months.

Eventually I compromised and said I would go through for leading hand, but only if I had a course. So, one Sunday morning in June 1943, I arrived at HMS *Mercury* at Petersfield for a 6-week course for VS3 (Higher grade). It was hard work, and I felt acutely my lack of sea experience. The exams were stiff and I felt unhappy about my efforts. I failed in practical coding, but did so well on the fleetwork, procedure, flashing, semaphore and coding instructions that I was passed Lower Grade. There was no difference between Lower and Higher in pay, but one had to be a Higher Grade before going in for Yeoman of Signals. I had no such ambition in those days so was quite satisfied.

My mind was more settled and I knew what I wanted now. On returning to the ship I volunteered for a sea-going draft, and no difficulty was put in my way. Two years on one ship was long enough, and I was young and keen to get where there was more excitement and danger. So I was told I could go on 10 days' leave with my kit and report to *Drake* again on completion.

It was hard to leave the *Forth* and Dunoon after such a long and happy stay. I remember especially Higgy, Buck Taylor, Arthur, Fred the evangelist (I heard the grievous news whilst abroad, that Fred had been killed in the D-Day landing), Windy, Jock, 'Fish-face' Trout, Yeoman Fynn and Chief Yeoman Stanbury. The Signal Boatswain Johnson was always good to me and I was given a good recommend from him on leaving.

No more would I see famous submarines going out on patrols, some returning, some not. 'The Admiralty regrets' was an all too well known announcement. What grand moments when we cheered in such submarines as *Trident*, *Sea Lion*, *Ursula*, *Sokol*, *Tuna*, *Thunderbolt*, *Sturgeon* and the [former] German U-boat *Graph* after successful patrols. We felt that we had played our small part in their successes. Then there was the other side of the picture.

The refusal of two submarines to sail, *Torbay* and *Simoom*, until more competent officers were put in charge. This was done in both cases. Or the mysterious failure to surface of two new subs, *Vandal* and *Untamed*, during exercises when no survivors of either boat were found. Or the mysterious sinking in Inchmarnock Water of a new aircraft carrier, the *Dasher*.

Yes, we may not have moved from Holy Loch, but we were very near to triumphs and tragedies.

So I said farewell to HMS *Forth* and Dunoon.

THE LETTERS (CONTINUED)

Sig. J.R. Dawson
D/JX232329, 33 Mess,
HMS Forth
c/o GPO Edinburgh
29/11/41

Dear Eileen and John

Thanks for letter received this morning. I think first of all I must pass on Norman's regards to you both. He wrote me a long and very interesting letter in which he said he may not be able to write to you for a while. He therefore asked me to send his best wishes and to say he is fit and has had a grand leave. He told me all about his girl at Derby and you can be sure that there is not a lot in it. I don't think either of us have changed much as regards our attitude to the fairer sex. He did not tell me much about his experiences in fact Mother told me more in that direction. He seems to have had a pretty grim time.

I am afraid you are wrong about Peggy and Ken, Eileen, as they have never been out together, although not through lack of trying by Ken. I understand he has been fighting for the affections of Pearl with the other Ken. He has been luckier with her and seems happier lately. He was not too pleased when I left home as he could not get anywhere with Peggy.

You need not worry about me at Christmas as I think previous money you sent me was a good enough present. You were too generous and you didn't ought to a done it.

I will not be able to visit Ronnie Saville from here, though I may be nearer in the future. We may be a little longer here yet, and five of us spend our time during the week undergoing special instruction with a view to higher rating. I think they are trying to rush me a little too quickly as I have neither the knowledge or experience (At any rate that is my opinion). We also have jobs to do on board (scrubbing out, colours and an occasional watch) so we are reasonably busy during the refit period.

Yes I received the packet of Irish cigs and I am sorry if I have not thanked you before. I have only been ashore once this week when I saw Anne Southern in one of the 'Maisie' pictures. As I have told you before, my mates are in the other watch so I went on my own.

Nothing else to say at the moment so good bye now,

From 'the baby' of the family.

Sig J.R. Dawson
D/JX232329 33 Mess
HMS Forth
c/o GPO [location cut by censor]
7/12/41

Dear Eileen and John

It was grand to receive another letter from you this morning and good typing too. I only type the envelopes as it would take me all night to do the letter as well. I don't know where you get the 'general' idea from, or perhaps you did not know I was in the Navy!!! Anyway I have to pass an exam yet before I move up one, so do not expect too much. If I fail this time I can always try again when I know a lot more.

I have not managed to get the suit yet, though I went to see if it was ready on Friday. It had not arrived so we had a meal, a game of billiards and went to see 'Pimpernel Smith.' My idea of a very enjoyable evening. We will probably have a similar evening this week, as 'The Road to Zanzibar' starring Bing is showing.

Don't forget to listen to Mrs Bretherick on the wireless, Friday at noon. She has succeeded where others failed. I wish I could hear the programme, but that would be impossible as we are only allowed the 1 o'clock news during the day.

No, Josephine is not writing now, so, as you say, I have blotted my copy book completely with her. A good job I think. For once I have no feelings about the matter, though my 'diplomacy' could have been bettered. She should have realised how I felt after that one night, without pushing in the rest of the leave. It only made it harder for me as I refused every suggestion she made. Things were made easier for me with having so much visiting to do as I always had an excuse.

I will not be home for Christmas though naturally I was hoping I would. All being well I should get leave sometime in January though one can never tell, I am sorry to hear about the parcel problem, but you will just have to grin and bear it.

I went to the Naval Service this morning in the canteen cinema and enjoyed it. Unfortunately our contingent had no hymn sheets, so we just had to hum and put a few words in occasionally.

I visited the dentist last week and he said my teeth were OK. He attributed my tooth-ache to cold. Anyway I have had no trouble since. I will have to close now as dobeying[4] and a bath are calling.

All the best to you both,

Love from John

PS Thanks a lot for 'Polo'. No, I had nothing to pay on the letter.

Sig J. R Dawson
D/JX232329 33 Mess
HMS Forth
c/o GPO London
15/12/41

Dear Both

I received your parcel this morning and thank you very much for it. Toffees and Butter-scotch [sic] are very tasty. I liked the baby card as well. As I had a parcel from home last week you can see how lucky I am. Included was the Friendship Book and it seems as good as ever. We started our 2 day exam this morning and it has been enough today to give me a bad headache. We had part of the oral this afternoon and that is what we all fear most. He had us in for about 45 minutes each and there is more to come tomorrow along with the practical. (You know Morse, flag-wagging etc) I am trying my best anyway.

I have got my new suit and it seems quite good. The trouble is if I pass, the badge I have on it (a new gold one costing 4/9), will have to come off. I should be able to sell it, though I have to pass first!!!

I did not hear Mrs Bretherick broadcast to her husband the other night, as naturally everything went wrong. I went ashore to

---

4   "Dobeying", "dobying" or "dhobying" was naval slang for doing your washing.

collect my suit before going to listen in at the YMCA. We were late in getting to town and by the time I reached the YM it was five to six. I asked one of the chaps to listen in on board as a precaution but he only heard the last 10 minutes. We went to see 'Too many girls' at the cinema but it was poor. Two nights previously we enjoyed 'Road to Zanzibar.'

As I have got my new suit I am now all ready for leave, and all I have to get is the leave. I am keeping on hoping. I hear that Edna has had her medical for the WAAF under the new scheme, so I have sent my best wishes. It took me ages to write a couple of sides to her. I hear quite regularly from Marjory and Pearl not so regularly from Peggy, and not at all from Josephine. Marjory is going full time nursing after the New Year and she said that she might have to leave Leeds. There is a chance she may come near where we might be (that's Irish). I certainly hope so.

I have heard nothing from Norman since he was home so I cannot tell you anything about him. Ken Standley has had to register and he has volunteered for the Air Force as his preference. I suppose you know that Sydney has now got a black Morris 12.

I have had a cold for quite a while but otherwise I am A1. It is naturally rather windy and cold up here. Recently we had our first air raid warning since reaching the UK but nothing materialised.

I have nothing else I can say at the moment so good bye for now and lots of love,

From John

PS sorry I forgot to thank you for the socks.

———————

Sig J.R. Dawson
D/JX232329 33 Mess
HMS Forth
c/o GPO London
19/12/41

Dear Eileen and John

I have not much to tell you this time, my main reason for writing being that you must always use the above address. I had to go and see the SO the other day about the previous address. The Censor had sent a letter to the ship saying that I must have given away its position etc. Naturally I said that it had been the general impression on board that the other address was OK and it ought to speed up delivery. He agreed with me on the first point, but the Censor said that it would mean more delay in the long run. The Officer was very nice about it and agreed that it was not my fault. So now we know.

Our exam for Higher Rating took 3 days to go through, and we all had a real grilling. The oral was the worst and four of us had approximately 1 ½ hours each with the examiner. We had all passed. The other chap was going through for Leading Signalman and his oral must have been about 4 hours. The Chief who has been instructing us said that at first, the Bosun was only going to recommend two of us to pass (including myself). The Chief, however, had a little talk with him, pointing out that there was very little between us all, and a little private studying would bring us all up to scratch. This resulted in us all going through. I am very glad because there would have been a little ill feeling in all probability, if the others had failed. I was lucky to get full marks in practical and that was the only reason I had anything on the others. I was a bundle of nerves on the oral and it was a good job he asked me the right questions.

As Daddy has been seeing to my Christmas cards, I have not done anything except to have my photo taken and written a short verse for them. I have been buying plenty for other lads when ashore, and last night alone I bought 3 dozen for lads not regular 'shore-goers.' We saw 'Lady Eve' at the cinema afterwards and really enjoyed it.

Tomorrow will be my first Saturday ashore for 5 weeks, owing to the fact that I did a sub for my pal once and early last week my watch was changed again. Now we are in the same watch at last, and we hope to have a good run tomorrow. It should not be too long before we leave our present port but I won't shed any tears over that.

I have nothing else to say so the best thing I can do is to wish you a very Happy Christmas and much happiness in the New Year. Cheerio and God bless,
Your loving 'brudder' John

PS I have 2 handkerchiefs from Auntie Ethel. She said she has heard from you and is glad you are both going on so well (I hope, we hope, everybody hopes). Goodbye now.

John Dawson

Sig J.R. Dawson
D/JX232329 33 Mess
HMS Forth
c/o GPO London
4/1/42

Dear Eileen and John

Many apologies for my delay in thanking you for receipt of telegram, letter, toffee and chocolate. Unfortunately, it coincided with our leaving port and I have only just begun writing again. We are now at our new base and apart from plenty of rain it is not too bad. When I passed for TO I fully expected some job more difficult to me when the ship really got cracking, and it has come true. Another TO and myself are working this business between us, and we are on our own, one day I work very long hours then he does and so on. The first day I did not like it at all, and no one explained much about it, and I was in a flat spin. I do not spend much time actually on board. Now that our food and shore leave problems have been seen to I find it quite a responsible and therefore interesting job. Once a fortnight I work all but 4 hours in 24, to relieve a 'WRN' for week-end leave. That is the worst part of the job but after tonight I will have done my 'day on' for a fort-night. They deserve it anyway (???).

Thanks for your Christmas and New Year greetings and I hope it has been a happy time for you both. Don't think I am trying to crave sympathy or anything, but unfortunately until Saturday I had rather an eventful 10 days.

Someone took a fancy to my gas-mask on Christmas Eve ashore, on Boxing Day I had an accident with something I was carrying on board and it went over the side. Naturally I had to go in the 'rattle' for it and I can assure you I had a very worrying 24 hours before I was relieved of the responsibility for it.

To complete a 'happy week' my tooth-ache came back. After a couple of days I went to the dentist again and once more he could see nothing wrong. I assured him there was and I assured him also of the exact tooth. He took my word for it, and did a steady ½ hours drilling before getting to the root of the trouble. The filling on top was sound and it was not until he had got most of it out that he could explain the pain. Naturally I apologised for my persistence about it, because I am afraid I had got a little impatient. It just happened that the tooth looked perfectly sound on the face, and he did not want to remove it unless I was perfectly sure about it. Anyway he has made a grand job of re-filling it, and when I get 2 more filled tomorrow everything will be fine. I hope all this has not bored you, but I was always good at telling others my troubles wasn't I? I am very fit now and quite content.

My pal Tom is leaving the ship so I am sorry about that. He is a great chap and everyone is rather disappointed about it. I will probably go ashore now with the third in our trio, who also hails from Leeds and he also is a very decent chap. He is apt to be too generous when we are ashore and I have to press hard to pay my share.

Keep smiling and I hope you are both in good health. 'We'll meet again' someday, and until then you will ever be in my thoughts, Lots of love,

John.

Sig J.R. Dawson
D/JX232329 33 Mess
HMS Forth
c/o GPO London
10/1/42

Dear Eileen and John

Just a few lines thanking you for your last letter. I have not much I can tell you. I am feeling fine and at last I think I have got rid of my tooth-ache. Today has been an unhappy one for our mess. Something was wrong with our food at dinnertime and nine of the chaps are in Sick Bay. I missed it by a real stroke of good luck, though I did not think so at the time. I was late for dinner and as it had not been kept warm, I just had the duff and a few biscuits. During the afternoon several of the chaps were very sick and altogether in a bad way. One other mess has had the same trouble and it is definitely a case of food poisoning. As a result the staff has had to be re-organised to meet the difficulty and we 'fit' ones look like being busy for a few days.

I have had two letters in two days from Daddy, and it is great to hear of his improvement. He seems very cheerful and delighted at the way everyone has treated him. I hear that Sydney also has been laid up with cold, so Mother and Kathleen will have had an anxious time. Daddy mentioned a very nice letter you sent him, in which you described your 'entertaining the troops.' Nice work.

Three of us had quite a pleasant run ashore last night. '40,000 Horsemen' and 'Charlie McCarthy Tec' were the pictures we saw, and the latter especially was grand entertainment. Once again it was great to have a warm bed (yes she gives us a hot-water bottle) and I really enjoy sleeping at Mrs Hayes. She wakes us up to tea and buns so it leaves nothing to be desired.

I am naturally looking forward to leave again when and if it comes. I cannot grumble at my present work as I am now quite settled and happy about it. The hours are fairly long, but it is worth a few extra hours to be one's own boss.

I hear rumours that Norman is nearer home, so I hope he gets another leave shortly. I have not heard from him since he was last home, though I have written two or three times. He doesn't write often but when he does it generally runs to about 8 pages so it is worth waiting for.

Are you both fighting fit? You seem to be managing very well and making lots of friends. I am glad to know this as my thoughts are always with you. It is a big relief to No. 9 to know how well you have settled down in Ireland, so carry on the good work.

Cheerio and oceans of love,

John.

Sig J.R. Dawson
D/JX232329 33 Mess
HMS Forth
c/o GPO London
19/1/42

Dear Eileen and John

Thank you very much for your last letter and I am sorry if I do not seem to have been writing to you as regularly as hitherto. I have not a great deal to write about these days, and naturally not the time I had before.

The weather has been rather grim during the last few days, being very cold. It has come to a climax today with sleet and snow. Not at all pleasant though once upon a time I would have thought it a very pleasant sight.

Just been listening to George Formby on the wireless. The first good turn I have heard for a long time as I hardly ever manage to listen to the wireless these days. George is a real tonic.

Yes my tooth ache has now gone and what a relief!!! I hope I have now no need to go forth-wards as you suggest. I would have liked to see 'Men of Boys Town' tonight, but I feel too tired after my 20½ hours on yesterday. (The last 16 hours on the run). I am glad such a spell only comes once a fortnight.

I have still been unable to pick up my rating, but in any case the envelope is addressed just the same. Why should I worry? (As long as I get the pay).

Incidentally I suppose you know that Norman is at present on leave. He has not done too badly for leave though he deserves it after all the sea time he has put in. I was wondering whether my leave would coincide with his but no such luck. I heard from him a couple of days ago, the first time for a couple of months. I expect his spare time is very limited.

Sydney said the family has not yet been to the Royal panto.[5] The visit is being postponed until I go home. I wish I knew when that was going to be.

I am afraid I have nothing else to tell you and I am sorry this letter is so full of nothing. Hope you are both well, cheerio and lots of love, John.

Sig J R Dawson
D/JX232329 33 Mess
Same Address
15/2/42

Dear Eileen and John

Thank you very much for your last letter. I must apologise to you as I am doing to everyone for slowness in replying. For several days now I have been extremely busy and I expect to be that way for another week or two. This is one of 5 letters which I am behind in replying to.

Yes I have just about got rid of my cold, but the weather is such that one can never be sure of keeping clear of colds for any length of time. The weather, however, is much brighter of late and quite pleasant.

---

5 The pantomime at the Theatre Royal in Leeds, which was an annual visit made by the Dawson family even after the war.

I have heard no more than you about Chrissie. She may be anywhere for all I know. Why should I worry?

I am glad you mentioned Norman and his 21st. It reminded me to send greetings in good time. Thanks also for mentioning 19th Feb, but I certainly have not forgotten Mother's birthday. That would be unforgivable.

My back pay looked and felt very good, and I felt very relieved to get it in my pocket. Believe it or not I had an egg the other evening but not on board. It tasted very good and I thought it was such a shame to eat it (liar).

You must be having good fun what with entertaining the troops and wall-papering. I hope you have made a good job of it. Jack-of-all-Trades.

Uncle Harold has written me an interesting letter giving me his views on what I should do after the war. I must have said in one of my letters that I expected having to start at the bottom again. He tells me why I shouldn't. I will have to travel around getting the orders in so as to get back to the peace routine. He says I will have to take on responsibility along with Sydney. Oh dear! I think I will stay in the Navy (liar).

I have seen a few good pictures this last week. 'In the Navy', 'Mr Dynamite', 'Fighting 69th' were the best but on the whole [*name cut by censor*] is rather a dreary place. Too many Forces and too little entertainment. One has to eat early, cinema early and then just walk around to pass the evening. There is a nice dance hall but that is packed out as a rule, and in any case we don't bother much there. One of these days I will be able to dance well enough to get keen about it. I have good pals and to me that is the main thing.

Do you hear much from Sydney? I don't and I often wonder if he is offended because I do not say much about him. I cannot because he never tells me any news about himself like Mother and Daddy do. I can only send him my regards and hope he is keeping well etc.

Now the 16th and I have received a letter from Sydney so I take all back I have said [*sic*]. Really must close and get my head down,

Lots of love

John

Sig J R Dawson
D/JX232329, 33 Mess
Same Address
1/3/42

Dear Eileen and John

Thank you very much for your parcel and letter. The chocolate was a real change from Bournville which I do not like much. I hope you have not been sending me bars and not having some yourselves. We are allowed one bar of Bournville per day, but as I am only on board once every 2 days for the 'dishing out', I do not often have any. It does not worry me as I am not all that keen on it.

After a very busy fortnight, during a temporary breakdown in communication everything is back to normal, and I am at last free to doby and write more or less at ease. I am sorry in some ways as I quite enjoyed the busy spell. Time passed quickly and it was good to get in plenty of practical and office work as well. Also instead of being on my own there were five of us during the day and four at night. Lack of sleep was the real snag, and on going ashore I spent most of my time in the pictures fast asleep. Last night, for a change, I was wide awake but the show was rather poor. I am afraid most of the pictures lately have only been second-rate.

I went to the Service on board this morning, only the second time I have been free to go for a couple of months or so. My pal goes on leave next Friday, but another chap (whom I knew on training ship) and myself have decided to go to Chapel ashore next Sunday evening, all being well.

As most of our branch has now been on leave, and three are going next Friday, I should definitely be going on March 20th. I know I really will be disappointed this time if I don't. That will make it almost 5 months since the last leave, so I am fully entitled to it. It sounds very near Easter so it would suit me fine. Remember last Easter??

I see you are having a Warship Week. Leeds made a good show, didn't they? Double the result for the previous War Weapons Week.

I wonder where Norman spent his 21st? I wrote the week previous to his birthday, but I probably should have written sooner. I had another letter from his parents. They write quite regularly.

We came across a weighing machine last night, so the three of us had a 'do' at it. I took my gas-mask off and I was weighed to

11 stone 2. I wore shoes and Burberry, not boots and overcoat, so it shouldn't be far wrong. I certainly must have put quite a lot of weight on since joining up. I would hardly say the food has done it as I do not find it good enough to eat much, so I generally have a 'reet good do' when ashore.

By the way the Olive Downing I recently mentioned is shortly to marry a soldier. I find she is 2 days younger than me, so it looks as if I am going to be an old bachelor (I hope not).

I hope you are both really fit and happy. My leave is all I need to make me A1.

Lots of love, John

Sig J R Dawson
D/JX232329, 33 Mess
Same Address
9/3/42

Dear Eileen and John

Many thanks for your last letter received a few days ago. I think I have already thanked you for the parcel you sent recently, and I am sorry if I was rather slow in acknowledging it. You've no need to tell me not to get married. Nothing is farther from my mind, though in any case such a thing as a woman is the first requirement I believe.

Yes at long last my leave is looking near. Unless unforeseen circumstances arise I will be home on March 20th for 10 days. I do not think I have ever looked forward to anything so much in my life, excepting of course the end of the war.

I must have made a mistake when I told you I had seen some good pictures, as the majority lately have only been second rate. It will be good to see a few first class shows when (???) I get home. I might just manage to see the Royal panto, though I am not really bothered about that. Mother and Daddy say they would like to return with me from leave and spend Easter up here. I am not finding it so easy to find 'digs' but we are going to make a big effort tomorrow night.

It does sound as if Sydney is not his usual self these days, and from what I hear he seems to be knocking himself out with work and worry. I will have to try and buck him up. (Big talk from the youngster).

I am glad someone else has trouble with Auntie Lena's letters besides myself. I haven't read one of her letters right through yet. I struggle through half-a-dozen lines or so then pack up. I make a note of any sentences which finish with a question mark, for replying purposes.

You need not worry about comforts for me as the better weather should soon be on the way. It is really grand today, warm and sunny. Quite a welcome change as it was very cold and snowing a few days ago. If, however, you fancy a little knitting, a pair of socks would be welcomed at your leisure.

We are allowed one packet of cigs a day, so at the present I am OK. Matches are very scarce, though we generally receive 2 boxes a week.

I have not heard from Jack Clay for ages, I generally find the magazine tells most of his experiences, as he seems to be a monthly feature. He wrote to me on training ship and I wrote back, so that is the extent of our correspondence.

The news is on at the moment. Pretty grim isn't it? Brighter days must surely come sometime. Always defending all the time. Never mind, what we have to say won't make any difference, so lets put our trust in those at the top.

I hope you are both happy at your work and in good health. Yes, let the girl next door pop in by all means if I ever come your way. I have struggled on to my usual feeble 4 sides, so I will say cheerio and all my love,

John.

Headingley 53237
Holmleigh
9 Cliff Lane
Leeds 6
23/3/42
3.15pm

Dear Eileen and John

It certainly is grand to be able to write to you from the above familiar address. I have been home since early Saturday morning when I landed in a city very dark and foggy. I lost myself in City Square (4.30am) so asked for the barrier and sat on my case waiting for the first tram. Another chap and myself missed our train at Glasgow at 3.50pm so had to pass time until 9.15pm. We spent about £1 each in that time so it was a good job we didn't have to wait any longer.

I find everyone here quite well and the weather has been very kind so far. Daddy spent most of the week-end at Huddersfield. I have just had dinner with him in town after which we spent an enjoyable 90 minutes at the News Theatre.

I am going out with Ken Standley tonight and probably Friday or Saturday. Daddy has booked for Royal panto on Wednesday and I may take Pearl. Peggy's to tea on Thursday as I can hardly refuse her invitation, and that's what makes it awkward if I take Pearl out as well. Keep it dark!!! I have no real interest anywhere, but I cannot say I dislike a little female company. I'm only human.

It was good to see the Blenheim crowd yesterday. Norman Darby and Leonard Briggs were on leave also. Mother and I had tea at Sydney's after they had been to No 9 for dinner. He seems much better now and quite cheerful. I have been to the Shop[6] twice and everyone is very busy. I hear Edna is getting married in a week or two. She seems to be even falling out of Uncle Harold's favour these days. There are many new faces at the Shop and everyone is going all out.

Syd and Kathleen came to dinner on Saturday, Mrs & Mrs Brooks following for tea. They left after a sing-song when darkness came, so the four of us went to Hyde Park. (Pictures not pub).

I am very sorry to have missed Norman by only a week but such is life. I have had my 'civvies' on today but my collars are too small and I have nearly been strangled. Back to uniform tonight.

Mother has gone to Blenheim this afternoon so I am going to make myself a really home made tea. Not just toast as I have been used to.

Apologies if this has been all about myself. I have a letter from you to acknowledge and I hope you are both going on as well as ever. Not seeing you for so long is naturally my biggest disappointment, but as you say we do know where we all are, which is a lot to be thankful for.

Look after yourselves till we meet again,

Oceans of love, John.

---

6   I think this is a reference to the Dawson factory.

An Ordinary Signalman

The following letter, although written apparently from the *Forth*, is a continued description of the leave at home in Leeds:

Sig J R Dawson
D/JX232329, 33 Mess
HMS Forth
c/o GPO London
Thursday 11.15am

Dear Eileen

I have just opened a P.O. Savings account and had a good hair cut, and as I have a good hour before dinner it gives me a chance to write to you. I think it is a good job I am on 14 days as I have been given a very large visiting programme. Cousin Ethel, Auntie Maude, Uncle Clifford, Mr & Mrs C Bennett and possibly Uncle Edgar are all on the list. That is, of course, without my own arrangements. So you will see that I am having a busy time.

I believe you enquired in one of your letters as to how I was situated as regards comforts and cigs. You need have no worries in either respect. I bought a few odds and ends home [*sic*] when I came last week, but I would have trebled them if I had had the money when at the other side. You really should not send money Eileen as all my money will come eventually, and I received a lot of it the day I came on leave (£10-10-0). Now for that burberry!!!!

As regards entertainment I have been to the cinema 4 times since we visited the Grand. Once with Kathleen and Sydney, once with Kathleen (Matinee), once with Josephine, and once with Marjorie. I have taken Peggy B home twice (after seeing José home first), so I have just about proved my 'neutrality.' In any case José is almost a back number now but that is a secret between ourselves. Ken St. is taking Peggy out for the first time tonight and he says he hopes it is only the beginning.

I had a grand afternoon and evening with Marjorie and Ken yesterday. They have a really nice house at Whitkirk with billiards and darts so I was soon at home. The 3 of us saw 'Escape to Glory' at the Ritz last night, after which I had supper at Blenheim.

I have only had one real glimpse of Sydney and the Brooks family (including Leslie who finishes his sick leave today), so I have been rather busy. I have managed to write 2 fairly long letters, one to Norman and one to Jack, though my idea of a long letter is probably your idea of a short one. I do not know how you manage it.

Yes Daddy and I went to see the match last Saturday, but Leeds had a bad day so I was a little disappointed.[7] We had Josephine and the two Kens to tea on Sunday. I had to invite the former as otherwise I would have had to go to her house. She acts like a woman of over twenty now instead of a kid of barely sixteen. I had quite a surprise I can assure you.

It was a very nice letter which Norman sent you, and I can quite understand your eagerness to keep it. Sydney has it at the moment but it will eventually return to its proper abode. No one seems to have heard from Norman for a while so he must be travelling about more these days. It will certainly be good when we all meet again.

I hope you are both keeping well and not working too hard. You seem to have quite a circle of friends now, and like myself, I expect you are finding that Ireland is a very nice country, or at any rate better than it is painted.

Well my news seems at an end so I will close by sending you lots of love, and don't forget to give my regards to 'hubby' (I don't suppose he likes me to send my love to him as I often seem to do). Anyway all the best

John.

Sig J R Dawson
D/JX232329, 33 Mess
HMS Forth
c/o GPO London
23/4/42

Dear Eileen and John

Once again many thanks for another grand letter. I must apologise for having sent your telegram a week early, but the idea was there. You seem to be having a good spell of weather. It is very cold here today and a real change after a very nice week.

I don't know that it is Wine and Women with Ken Davy, as far as I know it is just Woman. Anyway I was not supposed to know anything about it.

---

7   I think this must be Leeds Rugby League which was Dad's major sporting interest apart from cricket.

You need not have gone to any trouble to knit me any socks. I only made the suggestion as you seemed keen to do something.

Yes I feel sorry for heavy smokers with cigarettes and tobacco at their present price. We are extremely fortunate in that respect, and for goodness sake do not send me any 'fags' in the future. When we went to town last Saturday an old lady gave three of us a packet each and we felt very guilty as we accepted them. What else could we do without hurting her feelings?

Thanks for your remarks about Mrs B and Peggy, but I really do think they have been overdoing things a little. Anyway I have never given Peggy the slightest reason to think I treat her as any more than a good friend.

So you are Tommy Handley fans? I only hear him occasionally but I like his short programme as good as any on the wireless. We had a very enjoyable day in town last Saturday, our chief visits being to a big football game and a variety show. On our next visit (Saturday week all being well), we hope to see Vera Lynn. We went to see 'Hatters Castle' last night and found it sombre but very interesting. The acting was very good.

It certainly would be great if you could find time to pay a visit, though as you know it is hardly an easy place to get to. I have never forgotten that near miss at Derry, and as it turned out there was no need for my sudden 'embarking.' I often wonder where I would have finished up if I had stayed there a little longer.

I hear that Norman has been home again though I do not know whether it has been for long. I do not expect to see home before September, though I would naturally like to be home for my 21st. I only receive letters from Norman on rare occasions, and as he is now in England I am expecting one any day.

I am quite happy and very fit. I hope you are the same. Looking forward to hearing from you again,

Tons of love

John

John Dawson

Sig J R Dawson
D/JX232329, 33 Mess
HMS Forth
c/o GPO London
18/5/42
2am

Dear Eileen and John

I thank you for letter received a couple of days ago. I have not much to tell you but I will do my best.

The socks are a good fit and as good as any others I have got. You can please yourself about the gloves as I have no acute need for them this weather.

I did not hear Winston Churchill's full speech last week. We only heard the end of it at the canteen ashore. I see he was in Leeds yesterday speaking to a terrific crowd in Town Hall Square. I bet it was a real big day for everyone.

You will probably remember Higgy who was my best pal until he got a draft chit in the New Year. Well he rang me up the other night from a nearby port. He is married now and sounded quite cheerful. There was no chance of us meeting as his ship was only in for a couple of days.

We had a good day out in town yesterday, but as usual we tired ourselves out with walking around all afternoon. We saw a very good play entitled 'Rain' at night. Rather slow moving at first but on the whole quite good. The play was very outspoken and as the advert said 'not for the narrow-minded.' The two main parts gave fine performances and their acting was responsible for its success with the audience.

For almost a week now I have been doing the duties of leading hand of the watch in the office. This is the job I have always been dreading, but so far I have not done so badly. It carries plenty of worry and responsibility, and as I have had no previous experience I thought it rather thick to put me into 'gaffers' job straightaway. You see if anything goes wrong I have to take the blame even if innocent. It will do me good I suppose. I seem doomed to stay on board here for a long spell yet. I am sorry to have left the bridge again especially with the nice weather on the way, as I was just getting nice and sunburnt. (I know 'there's a war on').

I hope the magazine arrived though I am afraid I was late in sending it.

I now make an allotment of 10/- per week, so I know there is something being saved somewhere. I can now spend the money I do receive without feeling I am being over extravagant and selfish.

I have a letter from Auntie Lena to reply to, but as usual I am having a job to read it. I have to decode it in easy stages.

I seem to have written all I can think of at the moment. I should be seeing Kathleen and Sydney in a few days time so that is something to look forward to. Cheerio for now and lots of love,

From John

PS Do you ever hear from Norman these days?

Sig J R Dawson
D/JX232329, 33 Mess
HMS Forth
c/o GPO London
14/6/42

Dear Both,

Thanks a lot for your last letter written on the 5th. I hear that I seemed a long time in writing to you before, and I sent a measly letter with the magazine so I must try and do better this time.

Yes Ken Standley has now been called up in the RAF not Army. He volunteered many months ago and was then placed on deferred service after the usual 3 days away. Marjorie has not written to me for sometime, and I am a little surprised as we had kept up a regular correspondence.

I have had a letter from Norman. The lucky chap is on 3 weeks this time. He is on the right sort of ship, where the maximum amount of leave possible is given.

A small portion of your last letter was cut out. Probably about three words.

I am feeling fairly good now but I have had a rotten time with my health this week. I felt really miserable until Thursday when I visited Sick Bay and found the main trouble. I had treatment then went again on Friday. I seemed to be a lot better and Tuesday this week should see me taken off the list.

Today sees the end of my month as leading hand of the watch, as the Ldg. Sig. I relieved is back from leave. I am going back to my old job though I am hardly keen about it. I think someone else should have a turn.

I saw two pictures last week. 'Birth of the Blues' and 'Kiss the Boys Goodbye,' both of which disappointed me a lot. I agree with you about Bob Hope on the wireless, but I think he is hot stuff on the films and has no superior.

Now the better weather is here I certainly miss my sport, and lack of exercise is a big set back. With having been out of sorts I am anything but sunburnt at the moment, but my turn will come.

I hope you are both in good health. I am envious at hearing about blanc-mange for tea. Happy days.

I am always looking forward to the day when we meet again. It might not be so long. Cheerio for the present, from your loving brother,

John.

Sig J R Dawson
D/JX232329, 33 Mess
HMS Forth
c/o GPO London
25/6/42

Dear Both

Thanks for your last letter which, as usual, was very welcome. I am very fit again now after my few days off colour. I felt pretty miserable for that period as I had no idea what was wrong with me, until I saw the Doctor.

A pity your visit from Mother and Daddy has not been allowed, but it will be the next best thing if you can manage to do the travelling.

Yes, I heard from Norman, not once but three times. I keep hoping we may manage to see each other, as we are as near as we will ever get I suppose. He had a good long leave so he can hardly grumble at that side of the life.

I did not hear Dr. Underwood but I understand everything went off very well. I miss the services at home as I never seem to get the interest here. I prefer a walk if I do go ashore at all on a Sunday evening. There are generally three or four of us, so we are quite a happy little band.

August does sound a long way off doesn't it? It makes one think how much could happen before then. Best not to worry.

I have only been to the pictures twice during the last fortnight. I enjoyed them both, and with better weather on the way we only go to the cinema if we fancy the picture. The shows were 'Skylark' and 'Life begins for Andy Hardy.' Our prices have also made a substantial rise but these things have to be treated as minor details!!!

After very unsettled weather it is beginning to look as if we might be in for a hot spell, but one can never tell in this country. It generally manages to be either dull or wet when we go ashore. Today looks as if it may be an exception.

I still hear regularly from Pearl and Peggy, plus an occasional letter from Marjory. I understand Peggy is having her holiday week (or one of them) whilst I am on leave (I hope). She is not going away, so I trust she will be able to find plenty to do without expecting anything from yours truly. She is a nice girl, but the whole business is not to my liking, and it is so difficult to say anything when she has been so good since I joined up. She doesn't yet know how I took Pearl out several times, though there is nothing at all serious in that affair. I nevertheless find Pearl's letters of such a nature, that I have to be careful what I say when replying.

I hope you are both in the best of health and as cheerful as ever. You had better eat all the ice-cream you want before September, or should I say suck it? Anyway this has been rather a boring letter I know, because my news is very scanty. I'll hope for better material next time.

All my love,

John

John Dawson

>Sig J R Dawson
>D/JX232329, 33 Mess
>HMS Forth
>c/o GPO London
>6/7/42
>1.30am

Dear Both

Thanks for your last letter received a couple of days ago. I am replying during 'silent hours' as everything is nice and quiet.

I had a letter from Dad whilst he was in London. I have since had a word with them both and they seemed to have had a good time.

You can hardly be more impatient than I am for that magic month of August. It does not sound too far away.

Thanks for your suggestions re my 21st With the present shortage of matches a lighter would be welcome as would a wallet or purse for that matter. Don't lose any sleep over the job, however, as money is an always welcome gift. Talking of watches reminds me that I have been without since Whit. week-end. I dropped it several times before it eventually took the count. Sydney took it home for me and I expect it back sometime this year. If I had left it ashore here I would probably have had to call for it après la guerre.

Yes you thanked me for the magazine previously. This month's should soon be arriving.

Did 'Twinkle' remind you of that midnight broadcast? That was certainly good sport. Remember Arnold?

I do not remember the last time I donned a bathing costume. That is one article of clothing they dare not ration any more.

A couple of us went ashore on Saturday and spent most of our time walking. In between we saw 'The Last Round-Up' which was quite good. I don't expect I will be going ashore again for several nights, as I am not as keen as I used to be.

I have had a regular correspondence with Norman these last few weeks, but we have not yet been able to make any arrangements to meet. It will be rather a pity if no such opportunity arises.

Remember Higgy whom I used to pal up with before he went on draft. Well I understand he is now in hospital in Russia as a result of enemy action. It does not seem so very long since he gave me a ring on the phone and we had a nice little chat. He probably wishes he was back with us. Although he is active service (in for 7 years), he was never fond of the sea and generally saw his meals twice.

I had a long letter from Peggy last week and I must make an effort to reply I suppose. What a life!!!

Hoping this letter finds you both in the very best of health and spirits. Roll on my 14 days.

Lots of love,

John.

Sig J R Dawson
D/JX232329, 33 Mess
HMS Forth
c/o GPO London
13/8/42
2.15am

Dear Eileen

Many thanks for your cheerful letter received yesterday evening. As things are quiet at the moment I will try to complete this letter before turning in again.

I had another letter from Norman a few days ago. He is under training in the South and seems happy. I expect he will gradually cultivate that 'officer' accent which appears to be essential. As regards Betty I think you've been told the wrong tale. I have the idea that Norman is very keen about her as he always devotes a good part of his letters to speaking about her. I may be wrong but I think he likes her 'plentee much.'

Yes the party idea is definitely Dad's. I told him I did not want a 'big do' in these days owing to the many difficulties such as transport, food etc. In any case I do not like any sort of a fuss being made. As Dad seems set on something my last letter told him to do whatever would make them happiest so we will have to wait and see.

It seems a long time since I saw you and my one hope is that everything works out right for both of us. You should beat me home easily enough though I will not waste my time I can assure you. I missed the train last time but I hardly think I will be so foolish again.

This rotten summer seems to be general. I certainly do not remember a worse one. I was hoping to sun a little before my leave so that the Blenheim crowd could not say 'you don't look too well' etc, but the weather has let me down badly. Let's hope it clears up for 'Gala Week.' How long do you expect to be staying?

Thanks for gloves and socks waiting for me at home. Homemade socks last much longer that those we buy on board, and I am anything but useful at darning them.

I think Edna is Gloucester way but I am not sure, and I know I am past caring. Occasionally I have a letter from West Park. I always write back fairly promptly on those rare occasions so they have got nothing on me. I was very surprised to hear from York[8] a week or two ago, as I know they don't go much on me. He sent a couple of forms for me to fill up so there was a reason for his correspondence. I have never believed in making a fuss of relations since I left school and have no intentions of starting now.

Life is just about the same. Always fairly busy on watch (excepting during the silent hours), and still fed up with the same old routine. I am going to seek a change though before long, as I have had a good spell on here. Leave is the most important thing at present so I will 'bide awhile.'

I had one run ashore last week and I think I will have another tonight. I am rather surprised at the way I have adapted myself to staying on board. I used to be ashore at every opportunity, but now I am quite content to have an 'old mans evening.' I am always ready for sleep, which is only natural when we only get barely 4 hours every alternate night. A couple of hours in an afternoon on a form is hardly suitable compensation. I would be very selfish to grumble when other people are having to suffer so much, but we all have our little 'troubles' don't we?

I hope you are both in good health and I should imagine you are in the best of spirits. I am longing for the big day so until then. All my love John.

---

[8] Dad's Uncle Clifford lived in York, where he was an accountant.

An Ordinary Signalman

Sig J R Dawson
D/JX232329, 33 Mess
HMS Forth
c/o GPO London
4/10/42

Dear Eileen and John

Many thanks for your last letter, and, as usual, it was good to hear from you again. I am rather looking forward to the arrival of the Magazine[9] in order to read Daddy's version of the experience. He has already given me an idea of the contents, and as he would say 'the idea is there!'

Do you know, I have not heard from Norman yet. It was 5 weeks today when I saw him and I have had no letter since. Rather queer don't you think?

Ken Standley was somewhere Manchester way the last time I heard from him, but that was several weeks ago. I have not written to Marjory for ages, though I had no reason for stopping my correspondence with her. I still occasionally write to Pearl, Peggy and José, but the less the better as I never know what to say. Their characters are all so different.

After a week in the office I am back in the fresh air for another spell. I seem to be a real odd job man, as I represented our department in a 'tactical exercise' ashore during the week. I was carrying more gear than that, and I felt 'jiggered' afterwards. I wore a pair of sea-boots a couple of sizes too small, so it left me limping for a couple of days. Never the less the 'outing' was a change from routine, so I would be defeating my own views if I was to grumble too much.

I paid my third and last visit to the dentist yesterday morning. He is a new chap and very good. He filled the first of my 2 bad teeth without any grinding at all, so he was soon in my good books. I hope I can keep away from there for a few months now.

I went ashore on Thursday with a young Scotch [sic] chap in our mess, who has not been with us very long. My usual 'digs' were booked up so I meant to return on board. He stays with some friends, however, and I was persuaded to go as well. They were Mother and daughter. The latter being round about 50 I should think. Only poor people but very nice and friendly, and we were given a very nice supper. I daren't suggest any payment because Jock

---

9 The Blenheim Church magazine.

had warned me against it. Yes, well-to-do people have a lot to learn from such kindly folk.

I have seen two films this week. 'Hot Spot' was the first, which I enjoyed, the second 'Somewhere in Camp,' which was not so good.

My pal's wife has been up here for 3 days and he was able to see her every night. She went back today and he is now really fed-up. We saw them in the pictures on Thursday, but owing to a slight misunderstanding I was not introduced to the wife.

I hope you are both in the pink as I think I am. We have had a nice summer one day last month. Does that sound Irish? More probably Scotch [sic]. Anyway that isn't even funny so I will say cheerio for now and lots of love,

From John.

Sig J R Dawson
D/JX232329, 33 Mess
HMS Forth
c/o GPO London
29/10/42

Dear Eileen and John,

Very many thanks for parcel received yesterday and letter today. I am sorry I did not acknowledge it immediately, but I had a date for once last night and went ashore early. The funniest thing, however, was when I first opened the parcel. The name of the book 'Jumping Jenny' was a real coincidence as Jenny was the name of the girl I dated. Rather peculiar don't you think, as the name is not exactly a common one.

The eats have now been disposed of one way or another, apart from one orange which I will be devouring on completion of this effort. The socks are being worn and are a good job. Thanks again.

I heard from Norman earlier this week and here is his latest. On his last night at Brighton he met a girl he fancied quite a lot. He said he would have been 'nuts' about her 12 months ago but meeting Betty has altered things. Then follows a description of her, and also a few of her views. Anyway one thing and another led the subject to little me, without any girlfriends, or no particular one (Ha-ha). So he suggested to her that I might like to be a pen friend. She thought it might be a good idea so I have been given her address. I expect that means it is up to me to write first, but I have made no attempt to start as yet. I have other letters on my hands for the present. Seems rather queer to me that Norman should be taking this sudden interest in my future. There could be one good reason!!!

As you see, therefore, life is quite interesting for me these days. For a fortnight I have shared a room ashore with another chap on our 'nights off.' We only pay 5/3 each per week (3 nights), and for that receive supper and breakfast, two easy chairs, a fire if required and very cosy bed. I was not worried at first about joining in with the idea because I had got in the 'stay on board' rut. My opinion has soon changed, however, and everything is A1. It will be difficult for me to stay on board now.

This Jenny I mentioned earlier is a girl I have known for a long time. We have often talked together, but until last week-end I had made no real attempts to make any progress. Last Saturday four of us were having our 'once a week' night out, and I was for some reason in a bolder mood than usual when I met her with two friends. We talked for quite a while and eventually I took them all home (One was her elder sister).

I did not arrange anything definite but visited her at the GPO on Monday. Again we talked and eventually she let me have my way and the date was arranged for last night. So you will see she is a decent sort and not eager to go with anybody easily, as so many girls do these days. We went to the pictures last night and had a good walk afterwards. We made no future arrangements but her work makes it convenient for me to pop in at any time and try my luck. So you may have realised that I am more like my old cheerful self lately, and making the very best out of things.

The work is reasonably interesting and the fresh air part of it suits me a treat. A little cold perhaps but not too bad. I have heard nothing more about the Leading Sig. exam, and I am not worrying. My interest in further promotion is absolutely nil. No one here is interested in our welfare, because advancement in rating would probably mean good-bye to the ship. That would mean training new men and more work for the powers that be. Hence the lack of 'push' from the necessary people. It is the old story. Keep the man at his job if he is efficient and do not consider his personal ambitions (if any). In other words as far as we are concerned we will only be allowed to progress if it suits the department. This is only my view but at least I have the power to express it (I hope). Still I'm not grumbling, as I don't do so badly.

I must turn in now so here's wishing you both the very best of everything. All my love and I hope John did not miss the box.

Cheerio

From John.

Sig J R Dawson
D/JX232329, 33 Mess
HMS Forth
6/11/42

Dear Eileen,

This is just a short letter to wish you all the very best wishes for your birthday, now probably a few days ago. I will try and get a telegram off in the morning, but unfortunately I have the forenoon watch. Hence my sudden decision to write this and make sure.

    I have not sent anything to you beside good wishes. I dropped a hint to the folks at home to dig into my savings (if any), so I will not be too surprised if you say you have had a gift from me. Remember, I used to have a bad habit of not knowing much about presents received or sent.

    After quite a good healthy spell of weather it has broken again. We are hoping for a good day tomorrow, as three of us are having one of our rare days in town. We have booked for what appears to be a first class variety show, so I trust it does not let us down. (Orchestra stalls as well. Full elsewhere!!).

    I had a couple of letters this morning from girls I thought had forgotten how to write. Namely Marjorie and Josephine, so that means more and more to write. Even Miss Hampton and Miss Bayes pop up occasionally so I am afraid No 9 has to miss a few days when the rush comes.

    Anyway that's away from the point, and the point is your birthday. Doesn't time fly? So many things have happened to the three of us (Eileen, Syd and John) in the last couple of years. I don't think we are the worse for our many and varied experiences. The Navy has opened my eyes to quite a few things, but No 9 still holds by far the greatest attraction for me. We often grumbled at our life, but from what I have seen of the so called 'higher social class' I think I know where I belong and want to be. This country needs quite a lot of straightening out before we can say every man has an equal chance. I would not call myself a Communist by any means, but I think the Russians could give us a few ideas or examples in that direction.

I have not had my 'weekly' from Betty yet. Perhaps it will arrive in the morning though if Norman is home, as I think he is, then I may have to take second place.

I hope you are looking after John. Really must close now so all the very best and oceans of love,

From your young brother who thinks you his favourite sister,

John.

Sig J R Dawson
D/JX232329, 33 Mess
HMS Forth
c/o GPO London
9/1/43

Dear Both,

Thanks for your latest letter received yesterday. I think you will find our letters have crossed again as I am sure I have written to you acknowledging cigarette case, and also telling you my experiences at Christmas if any. I presume that the above information is now in your possession. I was more fortunate than you with Uncle Harold. I received a letter and P.O.[10] a week before Christmas, followed by a card and 10/- at Christmas. I think perhaps he was suffering from absent-mindedness.

As far as I know no news was heard from Norman at home for two or three weeks, but a cable was eventually received at the end of December. He spent Christmas in similar circumstances as the previous year.

I have not heard from Betty this week at all. A letter should arrive any day now. I have not received the photo yet as she was not keen on the one she had, and preferred to wait until she had a better one taken. No I did not send her anything for Xmas apart from card and calendar. I generally remember you to her when I write so I will make sure the next time is no exception. If things do turn out as I hope for my leave, I expect I will have some explaining to do to our people

---

10 Postal order.

not to mention the Brooks family (oh!). I will probably be glad when it's time to come back!! Incidentally the great day should be about 3 weeks away by the time this letter arrives. Just 21 days too long.

I am not well up in Scottish celebrations, but I am afraid I greeted 1943 in rather a dream. I had the middle that night so I was hardly full of good cheer, though I believe I wished several chaps all the best.

Yes I will definitely save one night in just for you. We will arrange the evening when the time comes.

Reference the baby situation and No 85 until your mention of it I had forgotten all about it, as I have heard no mention from anyone for sometime. K and S must both feel pretty rotten about it. I know I would. Such are the tragedies of life.[11] The Dawsons seem to have had their share in that respect don't they? Our parents have been the only fortunate ones really or have they??

Three of us went to the Baptist Chapel ashore last Sunday. Fred, our evangelist friend, took the service in company with several other sailors. The congregation was excellent (about 400) and the service was interesting if only for its originality. Fred and another chap I know each spoke on how they were saved or in other words 'what Jesus means to me.' I do not agree with them in many ways but Fred especially is very good as regards his frankness and mode of expression.

I will say cheerio just now. All my love and all the best to you both
From John.

Sig J R Dawson
D/JX232329, 33 Mess
HMS Forth
c/o GPO London
24/1/43

Dear Eileen and John,

I received your letter written on the 19th yesterday for which I thank you. I also heard from home and Betty so I was indeed lucky.

At this time next week I should be off duty for the first of 15 days. The past week has not dragged at all and I only hope this week passes as favourably.

---

11 'No 85' was the address of Sydney and Kathleen, who were believed unable to have their own children at that time.

My news for you is rather limited. I understand Kathleen and Syd are on about adopting a child again. Dad has advised against I believe, but he says Kathleen is not easy to dissuade once she makes up her mind.

I have finished with Jenny, for good I think this time. When I was first endeavouring to date her up I had a job to make the grade, because she had a local boyfriend who was in hospital. As a result she was not keen about going with anyone else, but I persuaded her that it was no good moping etc etc. As you may remember I had a couple of dates then stopped, and then a couple more (one only of which was kept). I rang her up a few days ago and she just said 'George is back.' I immediately said I would fade away, and she said 'don't forget to pop in and see me now and then.' I may and I may not. I don't know whether you are interested at all, but I took one of our WRNS to the pictures recently. She is good company and anything but quiet, but I hardly think there will be a repeat performance.

My best pal is almost due for a draft so I am now going ashore with him as much as possible. My present room-mate is in Sick Bay for a while so Buck has taken his place at the digs until we both go on leave. We have been good pals ever since he joined the ship (15 months ago), and I will be very sorry if he has to go. We have certainly had some grand times together, and never a row.

It is ages and ages since Sub Lieut. Norman wrote to me, so I am beginning to wonder if he has gone the 'way of all subbies.'

In her latest letter Betty (that woman again) said she is sorry I will miss her 21st party (6 boys, 6 girls) but she is not the only one. She finishes 5pm every evening the first week of my leave so that is a good start. She suggests meeting me in but I will be too late for that.

I must write home today or tomorrow and give them warning of my plans. I hope they see my side of it? Anyway whatever happens wish me luck.

I am glad you are both keeping fit. John will have to whistle when we have our phone call. You had better address your next letter to home sweet home I think.

Cheerio just now and lots of love,

John.

Sig J R Dawson
D/JX232329, 33 Mess
HMS Forth
c/o GPO London
21/2/43

Dear Eileen and John,

Many thanks for your letter written exactly one week ago. I have now been back 6 days but it seems much longer. I have not settled down anything like as easily as usual, but that is only natural I suppose. It would be peculiar if I felt otherwise wouldn't it?

Since I came back I have written to Betty 3 times, home twice, and a reply to a nice letter from Pearl. I hardly think I will be hearing from Peggy or José very often but one never knows. Pearl takes things the decent way and she was very nice when she rang me up at home. I saw José when I popped into the Primary but never had a chance to speak to her. So perhaps she was not very pleased.

I was only too glad to send you three letters when I was home as it was good to open up to someone. I can assure you it was not wasted time awaiting your phone call last Sunday evening, as we were in need of a few quiet hours after so much dashing around.

On seeing how Daddy took our problem at first until I explained things, I can understand what a difficult time you must have had in your courting days. He was very unhappy about the position for a few days.

If I do continue with Betty (and that is up to her) I expect I will have a little trouble in certain directions. She is not very religious as you probably know, and that is a bad start as far as Dad is concerned. It's just a case of how keen our parents are on such things. Her Mother and Father have never forced her in any way as far as Church is concerned. She does not mind going at all, in fact she enjoyed Mr Williams very much last week. On the other hand she says that *if* she should marry Norman or myself she does not want pushing there 3 times a day. She might prefer a quiet day or a walk. It is the old business of 'give and take,' and unfortunately Norman was all against it. I may be wrong but I see her point of view and admire her for it. I think such little problems sort themselves out if two people are really in love. Do you agree? Both Betty and her Mother have been worried about the religious side both as regards Norman and myself.

I agree that Norman and I will never be the same again. Of course it depends chiefly on him but for a while at any rate he will probably hate me like poison. Apart from this business, though, we have been rather distant in the last 12 months or so. It may have been imagination on my part.

Going back to Betty again I think she suggested spending more time with me because of her uncertain mind. She always told Norman about correspondence and of her accompanying me to a few shows even before the decision was made. She naturally did not enlarge on her remarks as neither of us knew exactly what was going to happen. I can assure you I was rather surprised when she told me her decision, because I told her my weak points quite frankly and pointed out the difficulties that would arise if she chose in my favour (though they were obvious).

She is very independent you know and she may easily change her mind completely. I have prepared myself for that, and told her that anytime she cools off towards me (if ever) to give me the tip right away. Norman did not seem to make any allowance for her doing that, and I am more than sorry, as his recent letters have been 'slushy' to say the least. Oh! The pity of it all.

Reference your question about choosing Betty whatever the circumstances, a) if it had not been for the war one cannot say what would have happened, b) if she had agreed to go with me and me only on the strength of that one night, I would probably have called it off, c) this leave put any ideas I might have had, that I was keen on her because of Norman right out of my head. Anyway you should be fed up of her name by now.

Life is just about the same for me and I expect the monotony will soon begin to tell again. I am settled in the digs with a nice quiet chap so I hope it continues that way. I have been to the pictures 3 times since I came back and I suppose I will continue in the same vein.

I hope you are both keeping well and I hope we all meet again next time home. Cheerio for now and all my love,

John.

This is the last letter in the file of letters until November 1944, when Dad had moved on in his naval career, as will be seen from the next instalments of his diary.

6

LEAVE, BARRACKS AND A FIRST GLIMPSE OF CRUISERS (HMS *SPARTAN*)

THE DIARY (CONTINUED)

My leave was probably my best ever. I had the female company of Betty and we became engaged. No one appreciates parents more than I do, but the company of a girl one's own age after 2 years with a batch of chaps, is something I had missed before. Whatever happened later, I enjoyed great happiness during that 10 days and we became engaged. (It was not my first leave with Betty, but it was our first real spell free from troubles which our romance had originally brought about.)

I left Leeds on August 10th for Devonport, anxious to see what new adventures fate had in store for me. After one night in *Drake* I was sent to the Signal School at Glen Holt Camp outside Plymouth. Here I renewed acquaintance with Pete Stewart who had also been on the *Forth*. I was only in the camp 3 days before being drafted to a new class of cruiser, HMS *Spartan*. Although still a TO and not yet rated as Ldg. Sig. I was drafted as a Ldg. Sig.

I had to travel up to Greenock again, but there was quite a large draft to different ships so we had plenty of company. On arrival at Glasgow another chap and I (both for *Spartan*) were told that the ship had been at Scapa Flow for a week and was working up. TYPICAL NAVAL DISORGANISATION. So we left by the night train to Perth and again on by rail and ferry to the famous and unpopular Scapa.

Then we were put onboard the depot ship, *Dunluce Castle*, as the *Spartan* was out for the day. We were feeling rather dirty and disconsolate by this time!!!

Several hours later the *Spartan*'s drifter called alongside for mail, and the two of us embarked with our kit.

The drifter entered the Flow itself and I gaped in awe at the battleships *Duke of York* and *Anson*, the US carrier *Ranger*, the heavy cruisers *Tuscaloosa*, *Augusta*, *London*, *Jamaica*, *Norfolk*, *Kent* and

An Ordinary Signalman

eventually *Spartan*. I was in quite a daze when I arrived onboard this modern fighting machine. There seemed to be lights flashing and flags flying in every direction. I reported to the Yeoman who told me I would not be required until the following morning. I was shown to the messdeck which was very clean as one would expect on a new ship. All the signalmen were continuous service ratings except two besides myself, and there were four boy signalmen (17 years of age).

One of the two HO ratings (hostilities only) was Jim Lightfoot, and I then began a friendship which grew as time went on. A Royal Fleet Reserve Signalman named Lawrence (Laurie hereafter) was also on the staff, and a Leading Coder named Pat McDonough (Mac). Mac did not join the ship until later; as you will shortly see, I mention these three, as their names will be entering into my story now quite a lot.

I reported to the Chief Yeoman next morning and he said I was quite a mystery. He had a full complement of leading hands, and if I were rated, one would have to go. So it looked as if the Navy had made another bloomer. At any rate he said the staff was not very experienced and he would be glad of any help if I did not mind being rated until circumstances cleared up a little. I realised here was a good chance to get off the ship if I wished, but I was so keen to settle down on a sea-going ship that I decided to remain onboard as he suggested. Whether I made a wise decision is left to the imagination, in view of future events, but as Jim said later, "If you had left, John, a beautiful friendship would never have been formed." Sentimental perhaps, but very true!

He gave me a practical test to note my ability, and I must have satisfied him as I was immediately put in charge of a watch, to the exclusion of two other TOs, one of whom became my second hand. For the working up period both visual and office were in 3 watches, which meant one never got a full night's sleep!!

My first few days were anything but easy, and I found little help forthcoming from the other two leading hands or TOs! I'm afraid there was quite a lot of jealousy between active service and 'hostility only' ratings. Anyway I was just beginning to settle down when the leading coder in charge of the SDO was taken ill and had to leave the ship.

Once again I was 'Jimmy Green'. No one else had much experience of the office work apart from me, so I was sent down there temporarily. I was very disappointed but determined to do my best. The six-week working up period was very busy, and consisted of going to sea almost every day and night for exercises with battleships, cruisers, destroyers, submarines, aircraft, gunnery target ships and occasionally on our own.

As a respite we sometimes went ashore in the afternoon to an ENSA concert, or had films on board once a week.

During this six weeks I was able to get to know the officers, the ship and my mess mates more fully. I never took a liking to the Chief Yeoman during this period, but I realised later that he was being hard-hearted in order to create an eventually efficient staff.

Toward the end of September our working up was complete, and we left Scapa Flow for Greenock. It was a very rough trip and I was sick for the last time in my Navy career, chiefly due to being below decks in a stuffy office.

I now realised that adventure was on the way, and I longed to get back on the bridge again.

7

HOME FLEET, BUT NOT FOR LONG??

We stayed in Greenock for one night only, and as we left after embarking ammunition, I could see the *Forth* in the distance. Our next stop was our home port, Plymouth, and we tied up at the emergency buoy. Mac was embarked from Glenholt Camp as the new Leading Coder and I was able to revert to my job on the bridge. After oiling we sailed on our first patrol in the Channel and Bay of Biscay. During our 6 days at sea we visited three convoys in dangerous areas, but on the whole it was all rather uneventful.

Our Captain did not seem to like signalmen, which meant that the officers were even worse. I soon formed the opinion that they were inefficient, and took it out of us because we got all the news before they did. The Yeoman in my watch was a good chap, and was scared of no man. I was sorry when illness made him leave the ship after the trip, but he was glad.

On our return to Plymouth both watches had 36 hours' leave, and I travelled to Leeds with a young coder from Middleton called Derek Kitchen. I had only a few hours with Betty, Mum and Dad before returning, but I told them I expected a longer leave in the near future.

LITTLE DID I KNOW!!!

HOME FLEET, BUT NOT FOR LONG

THE DIARY

PART II

In which I leave the shores of England for 25 months of adventure

8

MEDITERRANEAN, HERE WE COME

It was early October 1943 when I returned to the *Spartan*, rejuvenated by the short time spent with those who matter most.

The ship was now in the inner harbour, and the next few days were very busy ones for seamen and supply branches. We were a little more fortunate and were in four watches in harbour, working 24 about.

When off duty I was able to go ashore at 1.30 pm until 11.30 am the following day. My companion in chief was Mac as we were both in the same watch, and as Jim was a day man he could not meet us until 5 pm. One advantage of promotion!!

Whilst with Mac in those days I found he was a Catholic and was interested to hear his views expounded on the subject. He was always very sincere in his beliefs and not bigoted as other Catholics I have met. Religion does not enter into my story, as I never found much to be proud of in that direction in Navy life.

Whilst in Skegness Norman Brooks and I found a warm welcome at the local Baptist Chapel, and we had tea at the Church secretary's home on many occasions. In Dunoon I visited the Baptist Chapel, not too regularly, and also other places of worship when Fred was speaking. A Nonconformist, however, was never given the facility for regular worship on board ship, as only Church of England were regularly catered for. I went on many Sundays on the *Forth*, but my views of this and later occasions aboard are best kept to myself. I visited a High Church service in Tavistock near Plymouth one Sunday, but I was very disappointed at the end of it. Still I have always been willing to try anything once!!!

To get back to earth again. The future of the *Spartan* was very obscure, but most of us had no real expectation of a foreign commission at this stage. The rumour gradually began to spread that something unexpected was in the offing, especially when the ship was painted the lighter camouflage blue.

Anyway our worst fears were realised. Jim and I returned from shore one Sunday morning – to date Oct 17th 1943 – and heard we were sailing in the afternoon, and that we had mails for Gibraltar. We left Plymouth about 3 that afternoon, and it was very dismal and wet. The next six days were not happy ones for yours truly, as I had not even had time to drop a line home. This was remedied on our arrival at Gib and it was good to see the lights on at night. We had only one night in Gibraltar and unfortunately I was duty watch.

We left the following morning for Algiers, where a homeward bound convoy and escort were assembling. Amongst the escort was the cruiser *Cleopatra* whom we were relieving in the Med. I received the cynical signal from her, 'I have great pleasure in turning the Med Station over to you.' I would sooner have been on the Leeds station at that moment!!!

I had a run ashore in Algiers, but I formed a dislike that I never overcame. Too cosmopolitan and unfriendly for my liking. Our next stop was the George Cross Malta, which I also disliked at first but eventually it became my favourite spot in the Med. At that time Malta was acutely short of food, beer and other necessities for the average sailor. I know we were all very disappointed with the place at first glance.

A few days in Malta Grand Harbour and we sailed for Taranto to join up with the Admiral of the 15th CS, our new squadron. His flag at that time was in HMS *Mauritius* and also in company was the famous cruiser HMS *Orion*. So we realised that we had come to stay, and we decided to make the best of our new environment.

9

THE WAITING PERIOD, CHRISTMAS AT SEA, THEN A FLAGSHIP

We were told by the Admiral that the next few weeks would be spent in exercising with *Mauritius*, and generally acclimatising ourselves. This was rather a monotonous and trying period, especially for our branch, as exercises always mean a heavy strain on the communications staff.

I was agreeably surprised with Taranto, which had, of course, been the Scapa of the Italian Fleet. There was a good Fleet Club originated by a naval padre, and several free cinemas for servicemen. Unfortunately leave terminated at sunset, owing to air raids and fear of midget submarine attacks at night.

We fully expected to spend Christmas at Taranto, but Christmas Eve brought sailing orders. So the Captain informed us that our Christmas celebrations would be held at a later date. It was whilst at Taranto that the big disaster occurred at the nearby Bari. An ammunition ship had a mysterious explosion, which caused 17 other ships to be sunk or damaged with heavy casualties. We could hear the explosions and thought it was an air raid.

We arrived at Bizerta on Christmas morning, and left again at dinner time for Tunis. A few hours there, during which we almost ran aground, and then on to Gibraltar again. On arrival we soon realised what all the panic was about. The *Mauritius* was waiting to sail for England, and we were to take the flag temporarily. This was not at all popular with any of us, as it meant more work, plus a Signal Boatswain and Flag Lieutenant, not to mention the Admiral.

Anyway we forgot our troubles for a while and had a belated but hearty Christmas dinner, followed by an enjoyable run ashore.

Prior to this trip, incidentally, I had been rated Leading Signalman (Lower Grade). Whilst in Malta on our first visit, the Chief asked me if I would like to leave the ship. I said I had settled down happily, and would only go if detailed by him or the Signal Officer. He said that such was not the case, as he wanted to get rid of one of the two present leading sigs, who was neither efficient nor a good example. So he went, and I was rated by the Captain back to when I originally passed.

When the flag-staff came onboard we were put in four watches instead of the previous three, as the Boatswain brought another 6 signalmen with him. The leading hands were given a second hand each, instead of the previous routine of one in a watch with everyone else as dayman. My second hand was 'Bulldog' Drummond, who was only 18 and newly rated Ord. Sig. from Boy Sig. He was regarded by the rest of the staff as the chap who always managed to put his foot in it. Whatever he touched seemed to go wrong, but he was keen, and said he was glad to be on watch with me as everyone else seemed to be against him!!!

We were not a flagship for long, thank goodness, as, after a few exercises, we returned to Algiers and the flag-staff were transferred to HMS *Penelope* and later to *Orion*. We all heaved a sigh of relief on their departure.

10

PRELUDE TO ACTION

Whilst in Algiers the C in C Med., Admiral Sir John Cunningham, came onboard and gave us a pep talk. He said we were the most formidable fighting machine under his command, and that he expected great things now that every man knew his job efficiently!! These pep talks are a regular thing in the Navy, and the average sailor listens but takes very little notice.

In between Algiers and Malta we had a week in the dry dock at Taranto, to repair the damage done when 'hitting the bottom' at Tunis. Whilst we were in dock the *Aurora* limped in for a long refit, after a bad time at Salerno. It was my first glimpse of the Silver Phantom.

Our next stop was Malta for food and a full supply of ammunition, before making our first visit to Naples, recently liberated by the Allies. 'See Naples and Die' is a famous expression, but it never struck us as a particularly striking view, although Vesuvius was a sight to remember. At any rate there was no shore leave due to the typhus epidemic. One thing we did know, and it was summed up in one word, Action. We were at the Allies' most advanced port, and our initiation as a fighting ship was very, very near. My feelings were a mixture of excitement, tenseness and a little trepidation.

Eventually lower deck was cleared and our Captain told us we were about to carry out a bombardment further up the coast, in company with the flagship *Orion*, and zero hour was midnight the same day. No hammocks were slung that night and Jim and I got down on the deck, rather nervous, but keen to snatch a few hours' sleep before the call of 'Action Stations'.

11

MINTURNO AND ANZIO

On the stroke of midnight the bugler sounded 'Action Stations', and this time it was not for exercise. My station was on the upper bridge with the Chief Yeoman and other action personnel, so I made sure of my tin-hat. The next 4 hours or so were spent in slowly making our way toward the target area, which was to be Minturno, a heavily defended town which was causing some trouble to the Fifth Army.

When in position it was a case of getting in touch with the Forward Observation Officer ashore (FOO) by means of special wireless sets. For this purpose we carried onboard an Army Bombardment Liaison Officer (BLO), who worked out the exact targets by means of grid maps. At long last the dawn began to appear, communication was established, and our bombardment of strong points commenced with our modern 5.25 guns. After a preliminary burst the bombarding ship waits to hear the verdict from shore, and if a little off the target, a few adjustments are made before continuing. The marvellous accuracy supplied by the director, range-finder and gun layers were always a source of wonder to me.

This bombardment was essentially a test for the *Spartan*, and the *Orion* was present more in a supervisory capacity. A few wide shots from shore batteries were all the enemy could do in terms of counter attack, and before the day ended the following 2 signals were received from the Army:

i)   'Prisoners captured, report great damage and casualties due to your accurate shooting.'
ii) 'Minturno captured. WELL DONE SPARTAN.'

So our job was done in one day, and we sailed back for Naples in company with *Orion*. On the 9 o'clock news that night the bombardment of Minturno by British cruisers was headline news, but no names were mentioned. (*Spartan* was still on the secret list at that time.) We all felt quite happy that our baptism of fire had been so short and sweet.

Back at Naples but not for long. The Bay was full of ships of all types and classes. British and US cruisers and destroyers, minesweeping flotillas, store and supply ships, oilers, landing craft, MLs and everything to prove that an invasion was in the offing.

During the afternoon of January 21st 1944 our Captain again cleared lower deck and told us what was in store. We were to sail that night for Anzio where a large-scale invasion was to take place, with Rome as the big objective, 20 miles inland.

There were to be several beach-heads, three I believe it was, and ours was known as Alpha.

A mine-swept channel had paved the way for this vast fleet to enter enemy waters. The smaller craft left Naples first with their headquarter ships, and the supporting ships followed. 'Action Stations' was again sounded at midnight for us, and my job whilst going through the swept channel was to continuously report the twinkling lights at both sides, which indicated the newly laid dan buoys. It was a binocular job and lasted over 4 hours. Around 4 am we arrived in the area where our beach-head was to be established. Soon after, the troops and landing craft began to go in to the support of heavy gun-fire from one and all.

Daylight soon came and the Bay was a mass of ships of all shapes and sizes, all playing their part in one way or another.

As this was over three years ago I cannot give an authentic account of all that happened, as I was much too busy to worry about anything but my job. We were at Action Stations day and night, though during the dark hours our Squadron usually steamed 30 miles to the westward until the following morning. Once the beach-heads were established each bombarding ship had communication with an FOO ashore, and only in extreme urgency was any night bombarding carried out. In our staff one leading hand and 2 others stayed aft day and night, ready to man the after signal position in case of damage to flagdeck and bridge. This meant much more work for me, as one of the two Yeomen had to stay in the Wireless Office all the time.

The Chief and other Yeomen worked the Upper bridge between them, and I was responsible for the receipt and transmission of all signals to and from the ship, plus any interceptions we could get.

Prior to this, Jim and I had begun to draw our daily rum ration, and we were not sorry. Air raids, almost continuous day bombarding, a few near misses, all made signalling a strain. The *Spartan* was on the move most of the time, and after 3 days of this we were sent back to Naples for fuel and ammunition.

The rest was only momentary as all was done in one night and the following morning we left for the Anzio-Nettuno area once again. Our brief stay in Naples had at least allowed us to go into the mess-deck and see our pals once again.

12

THE END OF THE *SPARTAN* (1905 HOURS, 29TH JAN 1944)

We returned to the fighting at high speed, ready for the fray once more. The landings were going quite well in their initial stages, but, as the records show elsewhere, it was a long, long road to Rome.

Our return was on Jan 27th, and the first two days gave our guns plenty of scope. We had plenty of targets, several air raids to relieve the monotony, and many nearby shell splashes, but WE KEPT ON THE MOVE.

I had been kept extremely busy, and to give us a little rest I exchanged jobs with the other Leading Sig. aft. I was so bored just watching, that I exchanged after only half a day. To make things a little easier for the rest of the signal staff, Chief told me to let each one have a couple of hours' sleep, as far as the work allowed. It was whilst I was having my two-hour spell at dusk on the 28th, that the destroyer *Janus* was sunk by a glider-bomb not very far from us. The only other casualty which we had previously seen of any size, was on the first day when *Palomares* struck a mine, but she was able to limp back to Naples.

This glider-bomb was a new thing making a first appearance in warfare. It was a fair sized bomb, radio-controlled and hard to discern in its approach.

The night of Jan 28th was spent 30 miles out as previously, with the other cruisers in our sector, *Orion*, *Dido* and *Delhi*. On the morning of the 29th the Admiral informed us that he was leaving in *Orion* for Naples, leaving *Spartan* in charge for bombardment in the sector, under the supreme orders of the American Admiral in the headquarters' ship *Biscayne*, which was at anchor very close in.

It was our busiest day, as we heard that Fleet minesweepers, bravely trying to sweep a channel, were meeting heavy firing from shore batteries further up the coast. With the destroyers *Jervis* and

Laforey in company we spent most of the day bombarding batteries, radar and wireless stations on shore. The reports from shore indicated that our shooting was good. We had several near misses but *seemed* to bear a charmed life!!!

All day long we had been keeping in visual touch by 20" SP with the main forces, and around tea time we were recalled by the US Admiral in *Biscayne*.

The night orders were that, contrary to our previous routine, the *Spartan*, *Dido* and *Delhi* were to remain in the Bay chiefly for AA support in case of air raids. So, just before dusk, our Captain decided to drop the anchor for the night. We noticed that the *Delhi* and *Dido* did not.

The first raid was not long in coming, and we saw at least one aircraft shot down by LSTs further inshore. We thought it was great to watch, and awaited the next move.

Shortly afterwards, about 5.50 pm, more aircraft were heard practically overhead, and they were presumed to be hostile in the absence of orders to the contrary. Our Captain, always keen for action, and perhaps rather unwisely, did not hesitate to open up with everything we had got. I noticed that the other two cruisers did not immediately follow suit, but the *Biscayne* did. The noise was terrific and it was like a magnificent firework display.

Our nerves may have been a little on edge, but this gave us all an opportunity to vent our feelings. We cheered, shouted and 'shoot the so and so's down' was the main theme.

Then suddenly it happened. There was a terrific thud, and all of us on the flag deck were thrown to the ground with the force of it. This was at approximately 6 o'clock, and within a matter of seconds a large fire was burning aft, ammunition was exploding, and the flag deck was a mass of wires, aerials, tin-hats etc.

A quick test showed that the electricity was off, which meant the end of signalling. The ship was on a tilt of almost 40° to port, and it was a job to walk at all. Being at anchor left us a sitting target, and we hoped the enemy was satisfied. A merchant ship in the distance had also received a direct hit. There was nothing to suggest an 'abandon ship' order so we followed the motions of our Yeoman, who had been a survivor before. This was with one exception, as one of the chaps got in more than a panic, and along with others lowered the motor cutter and deserted the ship. The orders from the bridge were for all available hands to fight the fire aft, except the surviving signalmen (there were 6 of us on deck), and we had to go on the forecastle with Aldis lamp and battery, which we had been able to rescue.

On Chief's orders I flashed 'Request Tug' in all directions, and eventually a tug came towards us. Meanwhile several American patrol boats were standing by to collect wounded, but the Captain would not let them alongside as he still hoped to save the ship!!! The only man to get off then was the 'Paramount News' camera man, and he was last seen taking shots from all angles. He was only doing his job, but he was rather unpopular with us.

An hour soon passed, and there were faint hopes that we might get towed to Naples. Our forward guns had kept firing as long as possible, but prospects were not bright. I wondered how Mac, Laurie and the others in the SDO aft, and also the three signalmen in the emergency position, had fared when the ship was hit. I am afraid we all feared the worst.

Just after 7 pm by my watch the ship shuddered a little and began to keel over further still to port. I was holding the guard-rail with one hand, and the Aldis lamp with the other. It was now obviously only a matter of minutes before the ship turned over, so we all decided to go over the side. Bulldog was near me on the outer side of the guard-rail, and I had to wait for him to go, before I could clamber over. He seemed transfixed to the spot, so I threw the Aldis away and pushed him with my free hand. I followed within a matter of seconds, after discarding overcoat and boots.

The side of the ship looked dangerous, with a piece jutting out, but it turned out better than it looked. The water was cold, I suppose, and a trifle oily. I had my lifebelt on, and I appreciated it truly for the first time. A quick glance round and I could see the hulk of a ship some distance away. I struck out but was swallowing too much water. I had the sudden thought that I was nearer to dying than I had ever been, and then the 'will to live' saved the day. I thought of home and those I loved and I found a new lease of life. The next thing I heard was "Grab hold of this rope, Jack" which I did with great relief. I'm afraid I was too weak to pull myself inboard, but help was forthcoming in that direction.

I was then told to go below into the mess-deck. The name of the ship was *Weasel*, but to this day I know not whether it was a tug, trawler or patrol craft.

Then I made a foolish mistake. Cold, wet and thinly clad as I was I stayed on deck for some time instead of going below. I watched the last few minutes of the *Spartan* as man after man slid and eventually walked off the ship's side. She was right on her side and some were able to walk straight off into a boom vessel. It was like a wall covered with flies, and that was my last impression as I turned away, with more than salt water running down my cheeks. Whatever our views of the ship itself, we had all begun to settle down together, and, after all, it had been our home.

At last I went below and was soon acclaimed by Jim, Bulldog and some of the others. I could not hold a cigarette, and even the rum tasted like salt water. I had a few minutes' rest on a bunk, still with my wet clothes on, but we were then told that we were to be transferred to the cruiser *Dido*. So, with a farewell, a grateful farewell, to the *Weasel*, we went onboard *Dido*.

Photograph (source unknown) of a cruiser, believed to be HMS *Spartan*, before her sinking.

13

UNLUCKY FOR SOME, BUT NOT FOR ALL

Our first job was a quick shower with whatever soap was handy. I left my wet clothes in a corner, but never worried about them again. After getting rid of as much oil as possible I was given a pair of socks, underpants and overalls. I was too late for shoes, but managed to eventually get a pair of brown gym shoes.

Meanwhile I had temporarily lost Jim, Bulldog and the others, so I wandered around the *Dido* looking for familiar faces. It was good to see different chaps, of whose safety we had had doubt, but there were plenty missing such as Mac, Laurie, Kitty and my fellow Ldg. Sig. with the two youngsters aft. One of the two Yeomen also seemed to have unaccountably disappeared.

We were all feeling rather tired, a little shocked and rather depressed, so when I met Bulldog and Ron White we decided to go to the signalman's mess, with sleep the object in view. We managed to connive two blankets between the three of us, and 'got our heads down' under the mess-table.

Suddenly there was a terrific thud all over the ship, and Ron said, "Here we go again." But I remember saying that I had no intentions of having another swimming lesson that night. Fortunately there was no need. The Commander came 'over the air,' and said the slight noise (?) was a delayed action bomb just astern of us. The Captain then decided to proceed at full speed for Naples to discharge the two hundred survivors. We hoped there were plenty more as well elsewhere. Anyway we were not sorry to leave at that moment.

That night turned out to be really grim. I simply could not sleep, and was up at least half a dozen times either to have a drink, to be sick, or to follow the course of nature. I noticed several chaps were making no attempt to sleep, but sitting or standing rather vacantly, generally with cigarette in mouth. Ron was the same as me, but Bulldog slept well. Jim was in one of the other messes.

A good breakfast was put on for us the following morning, but very few partook of it. The salty taste was still too prevalent.

About 9 o'clock we were all fell in on the upper deck, a roll-call was taken, and then landing craft took us into Naples' inner harbour. We were then transferred to the famous pre-war liner *Winchester Castle*, now a trooper, and one of the few 'good' troopers in commission with regard to comfort for the troops.

14

RECUPERATION, AND A BIG DISAPPOINTMENT

Almost the first people we met on the gangway were Mac, Laurie and Kitty, anxiously looking for us. It was a grand feeling to know they were safe. Their views confirmed ours, however, that the three signalmen aft must have been killed instantly. The leading sig, Geoff Hartland, was 100% for the Navy, and I never saw a chap so keen on the job as he was. He joined as a boy and chose the Navy as a career. The other two, Crabtree and Brooks, were very young. 'Crabs' was only 17, and I always had a soft spot for him as he would do anything he possibly could for me. He was a wonderful whistler, and I well remember when he asked me if we would take him ashore in Plymouth, as he had no one to go with. We did so, and he told me afterwards it was the nicest night he had ever had. Brooks, I did not know so well. He was in my mess, but was fairly new to the ship. He got more mail than anyone in the staff.

Apart from these three, there were still 2 of our staff missing. The Yeoman was one, and the 'one who ran away' the other. They eventually turned up in Naples a couple of days later. Mac and the others had been brought back in the cruiser *Delhi*.

The *Winchester Castle* brought no complaints from us. We were 4 in a cabin, practically no work to do, and good meals. Most of us were able to get a few more underclothes etc. An ENSA show was put on for us the first night and it was possible to forget for a couple of hours. The following morning our Padre held a short but intensely moving service for those who had gone. Although it was voluntary, nearly all of us went to pay our last tribute.

We spent 10 days on the *Winchester Castle*, and Bulldog, Ron, Jim, Laurie, Mac and I spent a lot of time playing whist, knock-out and other 'passing time' games.

Eventually our Captain collected us all in the main hall, and said he had entreated the C in C Med to send us home, as a body, to commission another cruiser. He added that signals received confirmed that we would be boarding a trooper for UK the next day. We had no real fancy for another ship with the same Captain, but prospects of home were the big thing. How we cheered!!! The Captain started to say "I loved the *Spartan* —," then he broke down and left the stage. He had aged 10 years in 10 days.

I organised all night watches so that we would not miss any signals on the subject. It was an uneventful night and next morning we boarded the French trooper *Champollion*. What a difference. The ship was filthy, overcrowded, and the food rotten. Also there was no rum ration!

A Frenchman came down to the mess and he was asked, "Is there any *rum* aboard here?" To which he replied with unconscious humour, "Yes, there is plenty of *room*!!"

I was one of the unlucky ones who got a job. I was put in charge of a naval party detailed to help in the butcher's shop. It was a disgrace to see how much meat we had to destroy because it had gone bad. At least I did get good meals on that job, but we worked from 8 am till 1 pm, and then from 4 pm to 8 pm. After four days we arrived at Algiers, and saw the UK trooper *Strathnaver* alongside the jetty. After some delay, all our kit (which was not much), was placed on the jetty and we saw England getting nearer each minute.

To cut an unhappy day short, the news eventually came through that all was cancelled, and that we were not going onboard, apart from the majority of our officers. What a blow it was!!! Our feelings are better imagined than put on paper.

Most of the chaps went ashore to drown their sorrows, but *we* stayed on *Champollion*, and watched the *Strathnaver* sail for blighty. Some of the lads booed as she left to give expression to their great disappointment and disgust.

The mess-deck that night was bedlam let loose, and I almost had a fight with one of our chaps who came off shore a little under the weather. He apologised the next day.

It seems that the Admiralty was to blame for the sudden change of plans, but our Captain was very much at fault for raising false hopes. We also heard that the famous *Penelope* had been sunk at Anzio, and her survivors were going home instead. She had been out much longer than *Spartan*.

This did not alter the fact that this period, and the weeks following, turned all of us against the Navy for some time.

COMMENTARY

The landings at Anzio in January 1944 were known as 'Operation Shingle'. The aim was to outflank the German defences to enable them to be more readily broken through by frontal assault. Also Rome was nearby and the airfields round Rome would further assist the push against the German defences. Obviously the capture of Rome would also have political impact. In the longer term, the Allies wanted to attract German forces from the Russian front and from France, the latter to increase the effectiveness of the planned landings which followed on D-Day.

The Allies had already occupied Southern Italy during 1943. On 10th July they had invaded Sicily. On 24th July, the Italian Fascist Grand Council had effectively removed Mussolini from power. He had been arrested the following day, and a new Italian Government formed.

During August, this Government informally approached the Allies for peace discussions, whilst seeking to convince the Germans they were still on side with them. However, not convinced, further German troops flooded into Italy. On 3rd September, a secret armistice was signed. On the same day the British Army began to cross the Strait of Messina into Southern Italy. On 8th September the Allies landed at Salerno, south of Naples on the west coast. However, the Allies prematurely announced the armistice, leading to the Germans taking over Northern Italy, when Italy surrendered.

At Salerno, the Germans initially successfully counter-attacked and the Allies considered an emergency evacuation. However, more Allied troops were landed and, by September 17th/18th, the Germans withdrew from the Salerno area, pursued by the Allies. On 1st October, the British entered Naples, but the Germans halted the Allied advance just north of the city at the Volturno river. The German defensive success led to them putting more men and material into central Italy.

It began to dawn on the Allies in early October 1943 that the Germans were intending to stand firm and Rome might not be as easily attainable a target as had perhaps been thought. Nevertheless the Allies believed Rome was the vital target and indeed they needed to activate a front line north of it.

Progress was slow and fighting fierce. By mid-November, although the Volturno river was crossed, the Allies were well short of Rome and it was decided to halt offensive operations for two weeks to rest the troops. Meanwhile the British (backed by Canadians, Indians and New Zealanders) led by General Montgomery were seeking to progress up the eastern side of Italy. They faced not only strong German resistance but also bad winter weather. Although advances were made, by the end of the year, they were still well short of where they had hoped to be, and well short of crossing to Rome.

By January 1944, the Allies were still facing fierce German resistance, which now centred on Cassino. In early January the final decision was made to execute the Anzio landings, which were scheduled for 22nd January. This was the last date for availability of the number of landing craft required in the Mediterranean as they would be needed for the D-Day landings.

Churchill had been determined for the Anzio landings to go ahead even though there was opposition amongst the military, especially the Americans. Yet Operation Shingle was led by the Americans.

Anzio was then a small fishing port with a population of about 7000. Nettuno was a mile south and of a similar size. Anzio is about 70 miles northwest of Cassino. The British believed there were few German troops in the Anzio area. The Americans anticipated heavy resistance at the beach-head, as had happened at Salerno. In this respect, the British were right. The Germans were taken completely by surprise and initially the landings met no resistance on the beaches. The British landed north of Anzio and the Americans south of Nettuno.

Unfortunately the American General Lucas was a cautious man who wanted to create a firm base for the beach-head and so missed the opportunity to advance and allowed the Germans to build up their defences and counter-attack.

The landings had gone well. The weather had been clear and the sea calm. There were some 243 ships of various nationalities which had set sail from the Bay of Naples. They managed to avoid being spotted by the Germans as their aircraft were kept grounded by Allied air attacks in central Italy. The ships arrived off Anzio about midnight and the troops landed unopposed in the early hours. By next evening some 90% of the troops were ashore with some 3000 or more vehicles. There was still no sign of German opposition. Indeed, there was none on the road to Rome and Rome itself was virtually undefended.

However, this situation soon changed. The Germans, surprised by the Allies landing, were then surprised at the Allies not advancing. On the 23rd there were Luftwaffe and glider-bomb attacks on the landings and ships off shore. The British destroyer *Janus* was sunk, as was the hospital ship *St. David*. On the 24th the weather worsened but also it became clear that the German forces were amassing. General Lucas continued cautiously building up supplies, even though the troops were getting restless. Eventually at the end of January, the American and British forces began to attack but faced strong German defence. The Allies went on the defensive again and the Germans began to counter-attack and by 11th/12th February the Allies were forced back to their final defence line. The German attacks continued until 18th/19th February when massive Allied air and artillery strikes stopped the German attacks on the Allied beach-head. On 3rd March the Germans halted their attacks at Anzio.

In the meantime, on 13th February the Allies had halted their attacks at Cassino.

The Anzio position hardly changed until May, when the Allies moved forward again, still against stiff German opposition. Earlier in May the Allies inland had also moved forward with a view to joining up with the Anzio forces and capturing Rome. On 17th May the Germans evacuated Monte Cassino. The Allied forces met up on 25th May and in early June the Germans withdrew from Rome. On 4th June the Allies entered the city.

Anzio had led to huge losses on both sides and, due to cautious American leadership or, the Americans would say, due to lack of planning and British undue haste, its objectives were not achieved for months.

15

ALGIERS, MALTA AND A FRESH HOPE SHATTERED

THE DIARY (CONTINUED)

After leaving *Champollion* we spent a few days in the Algiers barracks, HMS *Hannibal*. It was a dismal time. It was very cold, we were still scantily clad and not given enough blankets for sleep. An ENSA show was the only bright spot. We had a glimpse of our old Captain one day, but he dare not face us and eventually flew home.

After about a week we took passage in the heavy cruisers *Cumberland* and *London* to Malta. Unfortunately Mac was left behind in a shore job at Algiers.

On arrival in Malta, all but the communication ratings went to a rest camp out in the country. They had quite a pleasant time there. Coders, signalmen, and telegraphists were sent to the communication barracks in Valletta, HMS *Camerata*. Kitty (the Leeds chap) left us here, and went home for a commission as Cypher Officer. He later went to the Far East, but not before he had called at Cliff Lane, and told my parents about recent events.

Whilst we were in Malta, the ship's loss was officially announced, and we were able to write home AND TELL THE TRUTH. It had been very awkward, writing home as if nothing had happened. Bulldog had told his Mother that he had lost all his gear, to which she replied, 'Harry, you should not be so careless, dear!!!' How we laughed.

We all had small jobs whilst in barracks, but on the whole life was much better. Our main grouse was lack of 'kitting up' and money.

I was otherwise quite happy in Malta, and 'our gang' struck up a lasting friendship together. Talks in the evening, billiards and a few film shows passed time pleasantly.

In mid-March a list went up which meant that all ex-Spartans in Malta (about 400 of us), were to be drafted to the famous cruiser

Aurora at Taranto. We were very happy to be going together, especially as we heard that she was either going to England or America for a refit.

On March 20th we boarded the French destroyers *Fantasque* and *Terrible* to take passage to Taranto. It was an uncomfortable trip, and we were not even issued with lifebelts. On March 21st we entered the harbour again, and saw our new 'home' in dry-dock, looking most unfriendly in her red-lead condition.

WE SOON FOUND THAT SHE WAS NOT GOING HOME OR TO AMERICA, BUT REMAINING IN THE MED.

16

HMS *AURORA*
MARCH 21ST 1944 – NOV 16TH 1945.
DOCKING, WORKING UP, BUT A HAPPIER SHIP

When we arrived onboard, the Commander, the 'Madman' as we soon called him, nearly had a fit when he saw us all in Khaki. The Captain, however, welcomed us but dispelled any rumours that we were leaving the Med. His name was Captain G C Barnard CBE, DSO and he always spoke to us at least once a week, on the progress of the ship, the war, and our own future prospects. We immediately felt at home with him.

The next month was the usual docking routine. The ship was very dirty, and full of rats, a direct contrast to the more modern *Spartan*. The senior Yeoman went into hospital ashore, chiefly as a result of after-effects, and I had to do his job, as no reliefs were available in Taranto. The other Yeoman did not like me, as Chief seemed to have more confidence in yours truly.

We all worked hard to re-commission the ship in keeping with its great reputation. The staff, with a few newcomers, was very happy. As leading hand of the signalman's mess and also duty Yeoman, I found that the next month simply flew. The leading hand of a mess is responsible for all the men in the mess (there were 20 in ours), the cleanliness, system of cooks, discipline and catering. An awkward job, as one has not to show favouritism or undue familiarity. If there is more than one leading hand, the senior one takes over.

New guns were embarked and gradually the *Aurora* began to look good. It is surprising what a difference the final coat of paint makes.

The *Aurora* is a two-funnelled light cruiser of 6000 tons, with 6-inch guns, dual purpose 4-inch, twin pom-poms, and numerous Oerlikons. Altogether a formidable-looking ship, but we wondered how she would go on in her trials.

By March 21st the ship was all ready for sea. (We hoped.)

An Ordinary Signalman

Our first run was to Malta, and I had to continue as Yeoman on the bridge, as the sick chap was by now too sick to return. We paid him a farewell visit, and he was most unhappy at missing the ship.

My first watch with Captain Barnard was grand. He asked me who and what I was, and I never felt awkward in his presence from that night onwards.

We stayed for four days in Malta, during which time we embarked food and ammunition. To complete our staff we also embarked another Yeoman, a fellow Leading Sig, and two Ordinary Sigs. Needless to say we had a couple of good runs ashore before leaving Grand Harbour, Malta. We then left on the 27th March for a month's trials in the Suez area.

The new Leading Signalman, an active service chap, was a moody sort and some of the lads did not take too easily to him as the new Leading Hand of Mess. He was jealous of the *Spartan* crowd 'ganging up' together, and this became pretty general throughout the ship. Our experience had meant the founding of a fellowship together, which seemed queer and suspicious to 'newcomers'. Anyway a few rows in the mess helped to relieve the monotony. Whereas I believed the best way to get the best out of a chap was to treat him decently, the new killick (killick is short for leading hand) was more high-handed. I think my methods were more successful in the long run, although there are always chaps willing to take advantage of a good nature.

For our working up period, which I will pass over briefly, we visited Alexandria, Port Said, and through the Suez Canal to Port Tewfik and Suez. It was very hot work, and both on and off duty I was able to get tanned to the waist, and below, as white shorts was our usual rig. Going through the Canal, 100 miles of it, was of great interest to us all.

After radar, gunnery, communication, and aircraft exercises we were ready for anything by the 20th May. Then on the 26th prospects of action appeared. A large German convoy was reported as ready to leave Greece for Crete. So, in company with HMS *Kimberley* and the fast French destroyers *Le Fantasque*, *Terrible* and *Malin* we left Alex about 5 pm. We were told that Churchill himself said the convoy must not get through. About 2 am we were recalled to Alex as Beaufighters had reported no signs of the convoy sailing. This same procedure went on for 4 nights, but we never had the surface engagement we all longed for. The 'Froggies' were especially disappointed. On the 30th we were given orders to sail for Malta, and the first night we missed, the convoy sailed. Beaufighters gave it a bad time, and Churchill sent his congratulations to them. We were extremely jealous!!!

A day at Malta and we sailed to Naples, a familiar place to us all. Restricted leave was now being granted, and we had runs ashore to Naples and the famous, highly commercialised ruins of Pompeii. As there was quite a large fleet in Naples Bay, the cruisers dispersed every night to various anchorages, so as to keep away from enemy aircraft and E-boats. Our favourite 'spot' was Castellamare.

On June 17th we returned to Malta, and did more exercises to pass time and get the ship 100% efficient.

HMS *Aurora* entering Grand Harbour, Malta on 16th October 1945.

17

PALERMO, REVIEW BY THE KING, AND ROUTINE (?) WORK

The *Aurora* was now a happy ship, and very presentable in appearance, despite her great work and eventual disabling during 1940, '41 and '42.

On July 13th we left Malta for a courtesy visit to the American Naval Base at Palermo, Sicily. There were many American cruisers and destroyers there and everyone seemed to get on well with us. We found American signalling quite different from ours, but we soon got used to it. As our future work would bring us in contact with them quite a lot, we had to learn their procedure and flags, which were quite different to ours.

I went on a sight-seeing tour in Palermo and we visited the Palace, Montreale Church[12] and the Catacombs. On other trips we went swimming at a nearby beach. After a very pleasant week we returned to Naples for the King's visit.

This took place on the 24th July, and British, American, French, Polish and Dutch men-of-war were all in formation for the big day. The King and high officials went round in a high-speed launch, and boarded several ships. It was very impressive, and we afterwards were told [*sic*] to 'splice the mainbrace'. As it says on the rum tub, 'The King, God Bless Him.' Lady Astor was on dangerous ground when she once tried to abolish the rum issue. (A tot is equal to ⅛ of a pint if neat, but is sometimes watered down to ¼ or ⅜ of a pint, at the Captain's discretion.)

The day after the King's visit we left Naples for Malta, and from there to Algiers. Mac came onboard to see us, and he was already most unhappy at not being onboard with the old crowd.

Our next job was unique but pleasant. C in C Med. was moving his staff to Naples, and our duty was to transport a party of WRNS,

---

12 This is presumably the Monreale Cathedral.

officers and ratings. It was a 24-hour run, and we put on a flag hoisting exercise for the girls' benefit. They all seemed to think life at sea was very pleasant, as long as it was calm!!

We arrived and left Naples on the same day for Malta once more. We arrived on August 1st and, by the large number of Allied ships assembling, we knew another invasion was imminent. It was amazing to see how many ships the Grand Harbour could accommodate. We were alongside two other cruisers, one British and one American.

Sailing orders were received for August 13th, and Captain Barnard, with map illustrations, explained the whys and wherefores of the invasion. It was to be on the coast, somewhere between Marseilles and Toulon.

18

SOUTH OF FRANCE, AND TOULON

After the Captain's speech, our Chief gave all the signal branch a lecture on tactics. As Free French forces were amongst the invasion fleet, all ships would have a code number (i.e. 2F5) for flashing purposes, changing each day. No flashing was to take place at night if possible, and only a minimum light in the shore direction by day. As the American ships were in the majority, we had to be patient in our visual work. (We always thought British signalling faster and more efficient than any other.)

The British cruiser force, the 15th Cruiser Squadron, consisted of *Orion*, *Dido*, *Aurora*, and *Black Prince*. The approach was again timed, so that the invasion forces would be on a firm footing as soon after daylight on the 15th August as possible. To achieve this the island of Négre[13] had to be softened up first.

So, at first light, the island [*sic*] was subjected to heavy air and sea bombardment, each ship having definite targets. This was considered satisfactorily done, and the various beach-heads were consolidated with surprising ease.

The first day's work was extremely successful, and at dusk the majority of cruisers withdrew for the night. *Aurora*, however, was still in touch with our spotting aircraft, and we decided to stay at hand for the night in case we received a further call to bombard. At first Captain Barnard was going to anchor, but when the Chief, myself and other ex-Spartans on the bridge looked aghast at the suggestion, he changed his mind. How relieved we all were!!!

Our minesweepers were busy clearing a channel in the distance, and I never envied them their grim, relentless but highly important work.

The night was quiet, and the next two days consisted of supporting bombardments as the troops advanced along the coast. On August

---

13 This is presumably Cap Nègre (not an island), which is some distance east of Toulon and overlooks the western end of the invasion beach-head.

18th, as oil and ammunition were low, we left for a nearby Corsican port, specially 'opened up' for this operation. Although so near the battlefield our two days' rest were not interrupted by enemy air-raids. They had enough to keep them busy!!!

On the 20th August we left for the operational area once more. We found, on our return, that the Army was on the outskirts of Toulon. On the 21st *Black Prince* reported defective radar, so she left us, and for four days we were the sole British cruiser amongst many French and American warships, including battleships. The British *Ramillies* was also in the bombarding. We had plenty of bombarding to do and we were always closer inshore than any of our Allies. The main trouble was a large naval 13.5" gun mounted in concrete to protect Toulon harbour. This gun was christened 'Big Willie' by our Captain, and received wide press publicity. With our tiny 6-inch guns we had many duels with this and other batteries.

The Americans, especially, seemed very reluctant to close in so as to engage these hostile batteries. Our Captain was quite disgusted at more than one of them, especially as they had 8-inch guns to our 6-inch.

For our bombarding we usually had two destroyers to provide a smoke screen for us. The US destroyers *Kendrick* and *Eberle*, and the British *Lookout* generally argued it out between themselves for the honour to protect us. It was a most nerve-wracking job maintaining visual touch with them whilst zig-zagging through the smoke, to the accompaniment of our guns only a few yards from the bridge and flag deck. And how I detested wearing a tin hat and anti-flash gear. It was important, however, and our Captain was emphatic that all in exposed positions should be fully protected bodily.

The afternoon was most thrilling on August 24th. The shore batteries were at their best, and *Aurora* and *Lookout* had to keep constantly on the move. Shells seemed to be dropping everywhere, and we were firing and zig-zagging continuously through most effective smoke cover, provided by ourselves as well as the destroyers. We began to wonder what the other big ships were there for!!!!

On August 25th, our big day commenced. The Captain, irritable at the delay in finally subduing Toulon, made a long signal to the American Admiral in *Augusta*, suggesting briefly that if all forces were brought to bear on the area, especially the island of St. Mandrier, which contained 'Big Willie', and most of the other batteries, we should be able to force surrender.

This was approved, and we were put in sole charge of the WHOLE NAVAL FORCE for the day. As this included two battleships, about eight cruisers and numerous destroyers it was a big job for *Aurora*. With our limited signal staff and equipment, it meant terrific work for us. It took us several hours to recall all the ships we needed, and for the Captain to pass on his plan of campaign. The American Admiral kept discreetly in the background.

The plan was simply this. At 6 pm, on our orders, all ships were to open deliberate fire at the island. The aim, to destroy the enemy and guns which were impeding the troops ashore. At 6 o'clock it started, and it was hell let loose. The noise was indescribable, and it must have been hell to the poor souls ashore. I often wondered how the French ships felt about it. 'Big Willie' was at last put out of action by the French battleship, *Lorraine*.

The slaughter was not without its humour. The *Ramillies* appeared on the horizon about 6.50 pm (the cease fire was to be at 7 pm), and frightened of missing her share in the proceedings, she opened fire at extreme range and missed the island completely. At 7 pm by means of flags and every available light we ordered the Cease Fire. Even the Padre helped us!!! All ships ceased fire with one exception. A small French destroyer, *Simoon*, had sailed from Algiers to see if Toulon was liberated, and joined in the fun even though completely ignorant of the operations. She had no liaison staff or orders, and our Captain nearly went mad at her 'disobedience'. Eventually, however, she behaved like a good girl.

During the bombardment, the relief cruiser *Sirius* had arrived, and after giving her the position, we left the area for Naples. We had fired 973 rounds in seven days, and fully maintained *Aurora*'s wonderful reputation as well as that of the Royal Navy.

Toulon was finally captured on the next morning, August 26th.

COMMENTARY
INVASION OF SOUTH OF FRANCE AND TOULON
Just as with the Anzio landings, so with the invasion of the South of France, there was heated dispute between the British and American political and military leaders as to its value. This time, the Americans demanded it whereas the British opposed it. Operation Anvil, as it was originally called (later changed to Operation Dragoon) would require a halt to Italian operations due to the diversion of troops and resources from there to Southern France. This left Central Europe to the Russians. It was originally intended to coincide with Operation Overlord but actually eventually occurred two months and 10 days after the D-Day landings in Normandy.

The Americans got their way and the invasion went ahead, in spite of Churchill pleading with US President Roosevelt not to proceed and pleading

BRITISH CRUISER KNOCKS OUT 'BIG WILLIE' GUNS

973 Rounds at Toulon

WITH only six-inch guns, the British cruiser Aurora went in to tackle " Big Willie," the twin naval guns of 13.5 calibre which the Germans had removed from a French battleship and mounted in concrete to protect Toulon Harbour.

Aurora (Capt. Geoffrey Barnard, D.S.O., R.N.) was the spearhead of the great naval bombardment which knocked out the harbour's big batteries early in the invasion of Southern France. In 21 shoots over seven days, she fired 973 rounds at gun positions, beach defences, mortar batteries, strong points, observation posts and troop concentrations.

Greatest target of all was the island of St. Mandrier, with its formidable batteries. Aurora could hardly expect to cope with " Big Willie " herself, though she kept banging away from time to time, so it was left to the French battleship Lorraine to administer the knockout blow.

The bombardment began with the attacking ships lying in a great arc to seaward of St. Mandrier. At the end of an hour's terrific bombardment the enemy batteries were all silenced.

Lieut. R. C. Olliver, of Plymouth, gunnery control officer of Aurora, said: " Towards the end one enemy battery of about five-inch calibre, but using only one gun, started rapid fire at us. We set at him and he stopped."

Liverpool Man

Petty Officer F. Day, captain of "A" turret, a Liverpool man whose home is in Plymouth, praised the often forgotten men who man the shell-handling rooms and magazines below the turrets.

" It was sweltering work for them," he said, " but I was not surprised to find how cheerfully they took it 'As long as we're helping the lads ashore —that's all we care,' was their comment."

Marine J. Burke, of Bolton, told of the devotion to duty shown by four musicians of the cruiser's Marines' band. When the shell-hoisting machinery of the after turret broke down, these four musicians, who normally operate the great ranging and training table in the depths of the ship beneath the bridge, volunteered to keep the turret working.

They went aft and helped to man-handle ammunition so well that the rate of fire was maintained. Aurora, which is adopted by Bradford, has a high percentage of men from Lancashire and Yorkshire.

Leeds man jumped from Janus off Nettuno

By a Y.E. News Reporter

A.B. Butters   **Signalman Dawson**

WHEN the destroyer Janus was sunk off the Nettuno beach-head—as announced by Mr. A. V. Alexander, First Lord of the Admiralty, in his speech yesterday—a Leeds youth, A.B. Jack Butters, aged 19, of Wesley-road, Armley, was among the survivors

He has just been home on survivors' leave.

He said he saved himself by quickly jumping into the sea and swimming away from the ship.

By joining the Navy last Easter, Jack Butters achieved his life-long ambition. He attended Armley National School and was formerly employed by Leeds Industrial Co-operative Society.

Another Leeds man who was in the Nettuno beach-head landing is Leading Signalman John R. Dawson, aged 22, of Cliff-lane.

He was in the Spartan in the action in which she was sunk His parents Mr. and Mrs F. Dawson, have received a cable to say that their son is well and fit and is now at Malta

---

Cuttings from 'Yorkshire Evening News' reporting the survival of John Dawson on the sinking of HMS *Spartan* and reporting HMS *Aurora*'s actions at Toulon covered in the Diary.

with Eisenhower, the Supreme Commander, at meetings which Eisenhower later described as some of the most trying of the war.

Operation Dragoon proceeded largely with American and French forces, enabling French-led troops to play a key role in the liberation of their country. The first troops landed at 0800 hours on 15th August 1944, after the softening up of the cape of Nègre by heavy air and sea bombardment, in which HMS *Aurora* was involved. The beach-heads were consolidated easily.

Naval operations were under the British control of Admiral Sir Andrew Cunningham, the Commander-in-Chief, with contingents sailing from various places, including Malta, Taranto, Palermo, Naples, Brindisi and Corsica. There were six battleships, four aircraft carriers, 21 cruisers and some 100 destroyers, with nearly 500 transports as well as smaller assault craft. Command was given to an American Vice-Admiral, but over half the ships were British. Progress ashore was good and speedy, and by 21st August, Toulon was surrounded. There were heavy seaward batteries manned by the Germans, which were attacked by Allied battleships and cruisers, including the *Aurora*, as described in the Diary. The focus was on St Mandrier, where the Germans surrendered on 27th August, Toulon having been surrendered on the 26th.

By mid-September, French warships were able to sail into a liberated Toulon and two days later into Marseilles. Within a month of the landings, Allied forces had progressed nearly 500 miles and linked up with the forces who had landed in Normandy. Casualties of Dragoon had been 3000 Americans killed or missing with 1144 French killed or missing. The Germans suffered far more and had 100,000 troops taken prisoner.

19

FIVE EVENTFUL MONTHS IN THE AEGEAN.
SEPT 1944 – JAN 1945

THE DIARY (CONTINUED)

As a sort of climax to the South of France work, the American C in C of the whole operation sent the following signal to C in C Med: 'I consider that the Commanding Officer of HMS *Aurora* displayed fine qualities of leadership and great aggressiveness during the invasion of Southern France in general, and off St Mandrier on August 25th in particular.' We received a signal also from the French Admiral, complimenting our communication staff on their excellent work throughout. Later our Captain was awarded a bar to his DSO, the Chief Yeoman a bar to his DSM, the Chief Telegraphist a DSM. So we all felt that we had done our duty nobly.

Following this operation we had short visits to Naples and Malta, and, of course, ammunitioned ship. On September 9th we left Naples for Alexandria, where we were detailed to report to *Black Prince* for work in the Aegean, under the orders of the Flag Officer ashore, Vice-Admiral Tennant.

This was our first real opportunity to form our opinions of Alex and the Egyptians. The centre of the city is quite attractive and not lacking in entertainment, food and shopping facilities. (If not served with 3 eggs with a meal, one sent for the manager!!) The Egyptians, however, I found to be very shifty and not in the least reliable. There is no middle class. One is either very rich and aloof, or beggarly and living or existing in filth and poverty.

On September 15th we left Alex for Crete, for which the Navy had lost many ships and men in her heroic defence. We wandered around this area for several days, and I don't think we did much bombarding. It was more a reconnoitre with an eye to the future. I do remember that on our return journey we sighted two Ju 88s within half an hour, both at short range and flying low. The first one fired recognition signals, mistaking us to be German, but our gun crews must have been dreamy, as we were unable to shoot either of them down and they both escaped. Our Captain was not at all pleased!!!! He was not approachable for the rest of the day, and the Gunnery Officer must have wished he was back in his pork-butchers shop at Brighton!! We returned to Alex on Sept 19th, and remained there for 11 days, preparing for action to come. Then came over a month of almost continuous excitement.

We left Alex on Sept 30th with a force of destroyers, and proceeded to a rendezvous off Crete, where we met the Carrier Admiral in the cruiser *Royalist* and several escort carriers. The next few days were spent in aircraft 'sorties' by day, and blockading by night from Crete to Rhodes. Orders for us were that stopping the enemy from leaving Crete by night was the main thing, but bombarding was allowed if excess use of the aerodrome was noticed. This proved to be the case, and our Captain wasted no time. After a mild panic shortly after midnight, when we chased a surface contact at high speed, and found the 'enemy' to be one of our destroyers, we settled down to disorganising the withdrawal of troops from Maleme aerodrome.

We began about 1 am (I had the middle watch), by firing star-shell to illuminate our target and also surprise the enemy. This is certainly what happened, as the enemy fired tracer at what they thought were British aircraft!!! Then we fired 50 broadsides in quick succession, which in all meant 300 rounds!!! The din and glare on the bridge was terrific, and I was relieved when we finished. To complete the panic ashore we dropped smoke-floats as we disappeared, to give the impression of an invasion. Quite a hectic night.

The following day we had a look around the island of Levitha, and suggested to the Admiral that we should go closer ashore to view the signs of enemy batteries and forces. The suggestion was not approved so we reluctantly withdrew. He said a lucky shell might deprive him of our help!!!

Late on October 3rd the *Royalist* left the area with some of the Task Force for Alex. We stayed, along with the carrier *Hunter*, and several destroyers. Can you guess what happened the following day? Yes, we went to have another look at Levitha, because, after all, we were now in charge of the party.

Aircraft were flown off *Hunter* to spy out the land. They reported no sign of enemy troops, only a few goats near the lighthouse. This pleased, but surprised the Captain, so he decided on a bombardment on the east side of the island, especially on the lighthouse which might have been the W/T or signal station, and another white building nearer the centre of the visible land. So the destroyer *Catterick* and *Aurora* had a firing competition, chiefly with our 4-inch guns. I think we just about came out best, and our aircraft supplemented the bombardment by low-level dive-bombing. We also had a go at other possible wireless stations with our 6-inch. Eventually we ordered 'cease fire' and the Captain had a few minutes' soliloquy. Then with alarming suddenness he created action.

Marines, signalmen from onboard us, and a seaman landing party from the *Catterick*, were to proceed inshore in boats and make a landing near the lighthouse. One marine had a wireless set (Army type) to maintain communication where V/S[14] would not be possible.

Everything ran smoothly at first, and through messages received, it seemed that the island was almost ours. Almost two thirds of the island was in our hands, when we were suddenly informed that the enemy, who presumably were in concrete emplacements, had suddenly opened up with 6-inch mortars on our weakly-armed party. They were finding it impossible to advance, and suggested withdrawal. Our 'Cap' said no, asked for the enemy's approximate positions, and then we had a good bang at them with our 6-inch.

It gave them a shaking up, but our men were only armed with rifles, and it looked to be a case of 'so near and yet so far'. Eventually it was reluctantly decided to recall our party, as darkness was threatening. We were disappointed, as our rival *Black Prince* was due to relieve us the following day, and we had hoped to have one island less for her to worry about.

Then came excitement from inshore. I was just on my way up to the bridge, the landing parties were returning, and it was completely dark, when there was a large flashing light directed towards us. The Chief read out the Morse letters 'Wir ergeben', which was 'We surrender'. Our German operator was on the bridge, and with his help, we were transmitting and receiving signals in German for well over an hour. A point of surrender was arranged, our landing parties returned inshore, and one at a time the enemy surrendered. The leader, a pro-Nazi, was sent to the *Catterick*, the remainder were accommodated onboard *Aurora*, about 80 of them. They were a mixture of Germans and Italians.

The casualties during the operation were one corporal killed, and about six others injured on our side, but the enemy lost many more dead, due to the bombardment.

The next morning we sent a demolition party ashore, and a Union Jack. By the time *Black Prince* arrived things were just about settled, and everyone was happy. So once again Captain Barnard had taken a

---

14 Visual signalling.

gamble which came off. On relief, instead of returning to harbour, we spent a few days nearer the Greek mainland, and did a spell of bombarding near Salonika. On Oct 10th we returned to Alex, but sailed again the next day and had a day's bombardment of Melos harbour, with the destroyer *Terpsichore*. The Captain did not think our efforts had been very brilliant, but we were amused by the BBC news later which claimed that *Aurora* had beached a large merchant ship and sunk many smaller ones!!! Who said the BBC were always truthful?

On our return to Alex it was once again a case of preparing for the next job. Oiling, ammunitioning, disembarking torpedo tubes, embarking jeeps and 875 soldiers spelt EXCITEMENT with a capital X? The rumour was that we were to be in at the kill for the liberation of Athens. When we embarked the Greek Cabinet and Senior British Naval Officer for Greece, it looked definite. Alexandria harbour at that time contained nearly all the Greek Navy, including their one battleship, and as we left harbour we were given a terrific reception by all ships, especially the Greeks.

Life in the mess-deck was really grim the next couple of days. Our mess, normally containing 18, which was too much, now accommodated 36. It was a nightmare to the other leading hand and myself. Each meal consisted of four sittings, and one had to sleep anywhere.

As we neared the rendezvous we met more and more ships, and our Admiral in *Orion* was in charge of the entry into Piraeus, the port of Athens. The ever-faithful minesweepers had swept a narrow channel, and as they continued their work, cruisers, destroyers, launches, tankers, merchant vessels fell into single line ahead and slowly made their way towards Athens. The mines were an ever-near danger and we saw a merchant ship sink in 2 minutes when she unfortunately did not keep to the channel. One sweeper also sank and another one (the senior officer) was badly damaged and had to leave the 'show'.

We were astern of the cruisers *Orion*, *Ajax* and *Black Prince*. Several mines were sighted and each cruiser kept on firing down the line until they blew up. It was all rather exciting and tense, and when owing to further trouble with mines, all ships had to turn about whilst almost stopped, the Greek Cabinet Ministers made a signal to the Admiral regretting the delay in getting to Athens!! What cheek, and the Admiral replied that he was in charge, and had no intention of throwing away British lives for the sake of a couple of hours.

Eventually we stopped in a small inlet for the night, and entered the port of Piraeus on Oct 17th. All ships were soon surrounded by locals in their various small craft. After disembarking troops *Aurora* was ordered to return to Alex, so we had no rest.

Between Oct 18th and 24th we embarked a large crowd of Naval Commandos, and we knew yet more fun was in the air. On the 24th we sailed with a task force of destroyers and escort carriers, Melos being our target. Bombarding, aerial sorties were the order at first, and by the strength of shore batteries and A-A fire it looked to be a difficult job. Eventually our Captain, who was in charge, decided on a landing place and the landing party were ordered to prepare for anything and rations were to be taken for a week. One ship signalman was required, and four of us volunteered. Chief decided to send the one chap in our staff who was not watch-keeping. I complained, as the same chap had gone at Levitha, but Chief said he could not spare a leading hand, especially as we were SO present. So he went, I stayed. The party were led by a Commander Dennis, and our Marines supplemented his force. Communication was by visual and wireless according to conditions and desirability. The next few days consisted of following the slow advance of the party, who were relying absolutely on our bombarding for their progress.

Food was sent ashore by means of Greek caiques, manned by Allied Army Commandos who seemed to have caves and inlets all over the place. They were really tough guys.

One evening whilst oiling at sea from the escort carrier *Emperor*, our Captain was in very cheerful mood and he made very confident signals that Melos would soon be ours. On Nov 1st *Black Prince* arrived on the scene, and after turning the situation over to her, we steamed at high speed for Alex. After ammunitioning we returned to Melos and found a grave deterioration in the situation. Our troops had captured ⅔ of the island, but the enemy had dug themselves in amongst the civilian population. We could have finished the job by bombing and bombarding the town, but it was decided that no great need arose for such inhumane procedures, and it would only cause political trouble in Greece itself. So very reluctantly, our cold and hungry troops were withdrawn after having had a tough time. The operation had not been a success, but it all helped in the war of nerves.

On our return journey to Alex, *Aurora* called in at the recently liberated island of Santorini, to leave food, especially flour, for the hungry Greeks. Our Chief was asked to go ashore with a deputation consisting of Executive Officer, Padre, Paymaster Commander and interpreter. He told the Captain he was too old for such jobs, and I went in his place. We were given a touching welcome, and whilst the rest of the party went on mules into the town at the top of the hill, I stayed on the beach to communicate with the ship. It was awkward work on my own and as I received each message, I indicated to local boys that they had to be taken into the town to our officer-in-charge. They seemed to understand and were eager to help any way they could.

As our landing craft came in with the food, I had to supervise its storing as everyone seemed to want their share at once. Then a small boy returned with a signal requesting the presence of our ship's doctor as the local bishop was ill. He soon arrived and was provided with a mule (or was it a donkey)?

After an hour or so I received a mysterious document, with the words 'Follow bearer' inscribed. So I had to mount the mule with all my gear. It was slow, laborious, and painful progress, and just as we were within sight of the town I received another chit saying, 'Return to jetty'. This I did and the party followed shortly afterwards. One of the inhabitants gave me about 10 million drachmas, which I found out after was worth about 4½d. To the cheers of the people we returned to *Aurora*, happy in the knowledge that we had brightened their lives somewhat.

The ship arrived back at Alex on Nov 6th.

Life had been so busy during the year, that there had been no chance of examinations etc., except for signalman, and trained operator, both mainly oral. Bulldog and Ron White, both in the Navy as a career, were keen to take a 6-week course for VS3 Higher Grade, with the rank of Ldg. Sig. I had been a Ldg. Sig. for some time, but only Lower Grade, so it was a chance for me if the Captain could spare us. (Bulldog and Ron were now both trained operators.) I told the Chief I was not interested in promotion if it meant leaving *Aurora* for good, as I was very happy onboard.

Anyway I was told that I would return, so the 3 of us left the ship for our 6-week course and 2 Leading Hands were sent to the ship as temporary reliefs.

We left the ship about the 10th November and returned on the 25th January 1945. During that period *Aurora* had a week at Haifa, bombarded Rhodes, and spent 6 weeks in Salonika during the grave ELAS crisis. I understand that our Captain had a very worrying time, and had many conferences on the trouble with General Scobie, and also Churchill and Eden when they came.

During this period Bulldog, Ron and I went through a hard course in HMS *Canopus* at Alex. I was the senior hand in our class of 14, and I had many clashes with the instructor. He disliked hostility ratings, and I disliked the way he overworked us. 'All work and no play etc.', was quite applicable to us. On week-days we worked from 8 am to approximately 11 pm, with shore leave once a fortnight. We also worked Saturday and Sunday afternoons.

Whilst on course I was able to visit HMS *Nile* every Sunday morning for the United Board Church Services. It was a welcome change and the padre was always most interesting in a modern vein, which made his services a case of 'full house' every week. Christmas was better than we expected, but Boxing Day was a full working day for our class. I had to sell a couple of pairs of silk stockings so that we could go ashore on Christmas Day!!!

The exams were stiff and lasted three full days. We had definitely been overworked, and 5 failed out of the 14!!! Bulldog was top of the class, and I was second, whilst Ron just scraped through.

After the exams we were given different jobs to pass time until the return of *Aurora*. Bulldog and Ron were mess cleaners, but I was lucky enough to get an office job at the Port Signal Office. I had no duties in *Canopus*, but went to Ras-el-Tin, HMS *Nile* every day. I was in charge of the switchboard along with 2 sailors, 2 WRNS and 1 Marine. It was not overly hard work, and I got to know all the rumours and facts.

Several times we saw cruisers returning from sea, but the *Aurora* was a long time in coming, and it was not until Jan 25th that I saw a familiar silhouette on the horizon. The ship was flashing to the Port War Signal Station and when she made a signal V Aurora (from *Aurora*), I could have whooped for joy.

We rejoined that night and it was great to see Jim, Laurie and all the others again. A couple of days later we were all rated VS3 (H), which meant we had 4 leading hands too many. I thought I would be drafted, but it was decided to send Bulldog, Ron and the two reliefs. So Bulldog and Ron said farewell to *Aurora* and us after an 18-month friendship.

With my newly acquired knowledge I was put in charge of instructions in our staff. It was a job I always did with relish.

COMMENTARY
GREECE

Greece was a problem to the Allies. There had been a Greek resistance movement against the Germans and Italians. However, the movement consisted of various factions – Royalists, Republicans, Communists, and anti-Communists.

Churchill was determined not to allow a Communist takeover. Even during the occupation, the resistance split politically into two factions: ELAS, an army of liberation, dominant in northern and central Greece, and largely Communist; and EDES, which was completely anti-Communist.

After 1943, the Greeks spent more time fighting each other than the Germans, despite British efforts to work with them against the Germans. Meanwhile, the Royal government and King George of Greece were based in Cairo, but opposed by both ELAS and EDES.

When the Italians surrendered in 1943, the Germans initially had to put more troops into Greece. However, this could not be maintained, as the Allies took parts of Italy. They withdrew from southern Greece. A further complication was that ELAS captured most of the Italian equipment on their surrender and became better armed than other Greek forces.

Churchill continued to have serious concerns at the Communist threat in Greece. He had little support, not surprisingly, from the Russians, but also little support from the Americans.

In February 1944, ELAS took over central and northern Greece. EDES was in control in Epirus. The British arranged a short-lived truce between the two. However, ELAS had no intention of accepting the Greek Government in exile and set up a Political Committee of Liberation, openly Communist, in the northern mountains.

While the King of Greece was in London, the Greek Army in Cairo revolted on 4th April. There was also a Greek naval mutiny. The British surrounded and forced the surrender of the mutinous army. The King returned to Cairo and agreed to form a new Greek government, representing all opinions in Greece. On 26th April 1944, Papandreou, Leader of the Greek Social Democratic Party, left Greece to become Prime Minister and called a conference of all parties. On 17th May, it was agreed to set up an all-party government under Papandreou in Cairo and that ELAS should continue to attack the Germans in Greece.

Churchill persuaded Stalin to let the British deal with Greece as long as the Russians could have a free hand in the rest of the Balkans. The Americans reluctantly agreed but Roosevelt said he expected the British to avoid bloodshed in Greece.

However, ELAS were determined to cause a civil war as soon as the Germans left. The Greek King persuaded Churchill that ELAS had broken the terms of the earlier agreement. The British military mission maintained contact with ELAS, but with some trepidation, especially when the Soviet Union moved a military mission into northern Greece.

Churchill continued to make preparations to assist the Greek Government with military support, at least in and around Athens.

The plan was called Operation Manna and was due to be implemented by the end of September but had to be delayed as the Germans were still in Athens. At the end of September, both ELAS and EDES agreed to place their forces under the orders of the Papandreou Government, which itself would be under the protection of General Scobie (mentioned in the Diary) the British officer in command of Operation Manna.

On 4th October, the Operation began with British landings. The Germans pulled out of Athens on 12th October. On 16th October, as described in the Diary, the *Aurora* took the Greek government to Athens.

Meanwhile, Churchill met Stalin on 9th October and reached agreement on Greece and the Balkans. As the Germans withdrew, they destroyed bridges, walls etc. in northern Greece. ELAS, in spite of being represented in the government, continued to go its own way. The Greek government, backed by the British, had to stand up to the Communists.

THE LETTERS (CONTINUED)

> Ldg. Sig. J R Dawson
> D/JX 232329
> 27 Mess
> HMS Aurora
> c/o GPO London
> 6/11/44

Dear Eileen and John

My last letter from you dated 24th October was very welcome, and it was all very cheerful. I am sorry my birthday card arrived so early, but with the uncertainty of our movements and the slowness of sea–mail, I prefer to be well on the safe side. I expect Dad's will also be arriving a couple of weeks too soon.

I have had a very rare letter from Uncle Clifford (chiefly about money), in which he passes a pretty good judgement on Betty, which she has already reciprocated. With being so busy lately my writing has been very limited, and as a result I have hardly been getting so many, which has shook me rather a lot. Still there are no letter-boxes at sea, so I cannot help it.

[*Section scribbled out, presumably to avoid it being deleted by the Censor.*]

Yes I received quite a good share of sea-mail from you last time in, which I acknowledged. I got quite a few mags plus cigarettes for which I will thank you again. I have received a 'Leader' today.

I hope to have a run ashore tomorrow, though for once it will not be with the old gang. For once we have not worked into the same watch, so I expect to have new company, which will be a change. Personally I will not be sorry when we have a change of scenery (preferably in the UK somewhere).

I am keeping quite well and I trust you are both in the same happy position. I anxiously await news of the 'happy event', and I hope it will not be too stale before it reaches yours truly.

The last film I saw was 'The Adventures of Tartu' which I enjoyed very much. It reminded me of the occasion when Norman and I queued up for the balcony at Leeds Grand, in order to see a Robert Donat play. It was during that week, I believe, when your birthday show was 'Joan of Arc' staring [*sic*] Constance Cummings. It's surprising how some of these memories are so easily recalled.

I must do a little washing now, so I will say cheerio and the very best of luck to you both. Keep smiling and keep me informed of the latest,

Your loving brother

John.

Ldg. Sig. J R Dawson
D/JX 232329
27 Mess
HMS Aurora
c/o GPO London
13/11/44

Dear Eileen and John

Firstly, may I pass on my heartiest congratulations, to Eileen especially, and I am ever so glad to hear that mother and baby are well. I feel very proud to be an Uncle again and also to see that John is one of his names.[15] Thanks, even though I'm not the only one with that name. How is John? I hope he did not bite too many nails during the waiting period. (I mean John senior this time) I expect this letter comes much later than your other fan mail, but I wanted to make sure everything was going well before I wrote to you. My other hope at present is that Mother and Father are able to make it complete by a personal visit. I can imagine what a happy day that will be for you all. I only wish I could be there as well.

I am probably leaving the ship in a few days time with two others, to take a Higher Grade course. I have refused it many times, but after weighing up the 'pros and cons' I decided there wasn't much to lose. The pay will not increase but my personal satisfaction will

---

15 John Michael was Auntie Eileen's first son.

(perhaps). Anyway it will be a change for the three of us, and will help to break the monotony. So there will inevitably be a gap in the mail from both ends I suppose. Whether we return to the ship we know not, as one never knows what is going to happen in the Navy. Promises mean nothing as we know from the past.

I have been ashore three times recently, and seen some flicks for a change.

I am keeping quite fit, and feeling more comfortable now the cooler weather is here. I bet I would freeze to death if I were in England or Ireland now. It's going to take a little getting used to when the time comes, especially if a spell further east has to come first. I don't like to think about it (the move east I mean) !!!

It seems ages and ages since I saw either of you, and when I do manage to come face to face there will be a new face. How time marches on? I feel rather out of the family circle with these big events happening, though in spirit I often imagine myself on the spot as you might say.

14/11/44
Saw a good film on board last night called 'Hello Beautiful.' Sorry I didn't quite finish this but one has to rush to get a seat. No more news about our draft this morning, but it should not be long.

Once again thanks for making me an Uncle two fold. Here's wishing you all the best of luck, and Eileen especially a speedy recovery.

Cheerio

Your loving Brother

John

Ldg. Sig. J R Dawson
D/JX 232329
S.T.C
HMS Canopus,
c/o F.N.O Alexandria
Egypt

26/11/44

Dear Eileen, Mum, Dad and John

I trust this arrived in time to catch you together, and if not perhaps it can be forwarded. I was very glad to receive a re-directed letter from Dad this morning, which was welcome as I was not expecting any yet. The three of us went ashore last night after a grim weeks work, and as luck would have it we saw a lot of the chaps including good old Jim. He told me about Dad's letter. It was rather amusing yesterday, as I had written a letter to Jim in the afternoon but not posted it. I told him what it was all about so I have now destroyed it. He told us latest events on board, which included temporary reliefs (at least I hope they are). Their latest trip included a visit to Palestine, so I am sorry we missed that.

28/11/44

So sorry but I simply haven't had time to continue it. Last night it was 10.30 before we finished. I received a redirected letter from Mother yesterday, for which I thank her very much.

We have just finished supper, but I feel very little better for it. Rice is a favourite substitute for dehydrated potatoes, and I am not too keen. Nevertheless the food could be a lot worse. How is it for eggs in UK these days? We cannot grumble at a shortage especially ashore, and we generally have three each on our few days off when a run ashore is allowed!!!

On Sunday morning Bulldog and I went to the United Board Service, and it was a nice quiet service. There was no organist so we sang a couple of well known hymns as best we could. The most that could be said of it was that the idea was there.

I seem to remember asking Dad in a previous letter, if he knew a brush firm called Culmer's at all. Our Signal Officer on the ship had his father in the business, but I do not know the size or nature of his work.

I am glad my birthday card arrived just right for Dad's birthday, as usually I am either too early or too late. I'm afraid I have no idea as to Mrs Hunt's address, except that Fred lived in Oxford.

Well, how is John Michael progressing, not to mention his proud mother? It must have been grand for you all to be together, and I'll bet Mum and Dad did a bit of reminiscing on the way over. Time marches on and all that!! One of these days we will all be able to sit round the fire and tell our tales. We will need plenty of coal that night.

I have not heard a news bulletin for over a week, but I understand the War is proceeding satisfactorily. I notice that the United had their first defeat for many weeks on Saturday and Leeds had one of their rare victories.

I suppose more work is indicated now until bed-time! What a life.

Before I carry on the good work, I send my greetings to you all, whether still together or not. Give baby John a kiss from Uncle John please.

Cheerio,

Your loving brother or son (as the case may be)

John

In the top left of the following letter there is a message referring to letters received but unfortunately part of this is cut out so the only part that can be read says 'had letters from Derek Kitchen, Sid. Sorry I won't be seeing Mum and Dad this year!!! Perhaps next.'

Ldg. Sig. J R Dawson
D/JX 232329
S.T.C
HMS Canopus
c/o F.N.O Alex
Egypt
8/12/44

Dear All

Working on the assumption that the folks are leaving Belfast on the 15th, I am hoping this may just catch you all together. I have 40 minutes in which to get the job done, and it is the first chance

I have had of writing this week, apart from a letter to Betty last Monday. We are very busy on this course of ours, and any spare time is spent either washing or queuing up for meals. So please excuse the writing.

We are not even allowed ashore at weekends now, so Christmas Day will probably be the next chance the three of us will have of relaxation. The exams come a couple of days after I believe. We had a very stiff paper last Saturday morning, and I really thought I had made a complete mess of it. Our instructor marked them and said anyone obtaining 60% on his marks (and there is a section torn away and it then says 'to pass'.) Out of 14 of us the top percentage was 73, I was second with 69, Bulldog fourth with 62 and Knocker White about 44. So I was the only 'hostilities only' rating in the first four. We have another paper tomorrow, on procedure this time, so I must do my best again.

During the week I have been very pleased to receive four re-directed letters (one dated Nov 25th from Belfast), and the lovely Christmas parcel. Many thanks to all concerned and I think the rest of the class will second that as regards the parcel. I have distributed some of the brushes, and we all had a Manikin the other night. Instead of the Captain, Dad, I gave the Yeoman a nice big one. Glad to hear you have connections with our old Signal Officer, but I was not all that keen on him. It all goes to show what a small world it is. I rang the Chief up last night but he was not there, so I had a chat with Jimmy. I told him that we would like to go back on completion of the course, and he seemed to think that such was the general idea and that the present reliefs were only temporary. I believe Jim is at present suffering with boils, and one of the other has a [*section torn out*] I was rather jealous to hear the ship mentioned on the news earlier in the week!!

It really was grand to know definitely that your reunion at last came true. I'll bet it has been a very happy time for all of you, though Mike (sorry Michael) would not be much the wiser. I only wish I could have accompanied Mum and Dad. Never mind, Eileen and John, I will torment you one of these days. I trust everyone is in good health.

Bulldog and I paid our second visit to the Nonconformist service last Sunday and the guest Minister was Dr Leslie Church, ex-President of the Methodist Conference. He is touring the Middle East, and this was his first visit to Alex. I really think it was the most interesting sermon I have ever heard, and his illustrations were simplified and all the more effective. He said a great deal in a short time, and had very good hymns. His text, rather an unusual one he said, was 'He that gathereth not, scattereth.' (I think that is right).

Unfortunately my space is now filled, so I cannot say much more apart from a very sincere thank you for this week's gift. I am well but may be rather busy until the end of the month. [*section torn from letter*]

John

Ldg. Sig. J R Dawson
D/JX 232329
S.T.C
HMS Canopus
c/o F.M.O Alexandria
Egypt
5/1/45

Dear Eileen and John

I have not written to you for some time, not since Mother and Dad were with you in fact. I am sorry and I trust that you are both well, and also John Michael (which do you call him?).

We finished our exams last Friday and since then have been doing various jobs under the orders of the instructor, and the supervision of yours truly. This has included written work, painting, whitewashing etc so it has not been exactly monotonous. I have not yet heard what the future is likely to be for the three of us, and whether we are going back to the ship or not. Until a definite draft comes along one way or the other, I am commencing a temporary office job on Sunday next. The hours are fair enough, and the work does not sound too bad so I should be OK for a while, until something definite comes along. I expect Bulldog and Ron will be passing time doing odd jobs here and there.

The weather is anything but pleasant for us now, so it should be worse still in UK. After such a hot summer and autumn wearing only white shorts, the cold weather is very disagreeable, especially as we were never re-issued with overcoats or burberrys. I am playing football after tea and I will have to run about plenty in order to keep reasonably warm. It will be my first game for many months so I hope I do not let the others down.

After quite a strenuous 6 weeks course, it has seemed strange to have most evenings without any duties or work, and we have been trying to make up for lost time. We are not rich enough to go ashore, so on Monday we saw the film 'Journey for Margaret' in here, last night was a female ENSA show, and tonight I believe there is a Mae West picture.

I have made a dental appointment for next Tuesday morning, presuming I will still be here. It is about time someone had a look at my teeth as there are several needing attention.

Please keep it to yourselves (and I mean that) but Betty and I seem to have come to one of those awkward spells. I honestly cannot tell you what has caused a little cooling off at your end (or should I say her end), but at any rate there is 'summat up'. I do not wish to present my idea of the whole business, as it may be wrong so please let it suffice at what I have said. I think this long separation is having something to do with it. Anyway please keep it as a secret between the 3 of us, as I do not think it is very serious yet. If only I could get home I am sure I could straighten it out. I can assure you that my feelings for her have never changed, nor are likely to in the future. I only hope that everything works out for the best. I trust you will write to her as usual, Eileen, as I know she likes to hear from you.

Sorry if this has not been very interesting, but I am not exactly full of beans at present. I wish this blinking war was over, but who doesn't for that matter? I hope John is not working too hard, and that John minor is behaving himself,

That's all for now,

Your affectionate brother John (medium).

John Dawson

> Ldg. Sig. J R Dawson
> D/JX 232329
> S.T.C
> HMS Canopus
> c/o F.M.O Alexandria
> Egypt
> 18/1/45

Dear Eileen and John

After quite a run around your very nice letter and enclosed money arrived here a couple of days ago. Thanks very much, and though it did arrive a little later than you had hoped its usefulness was nevertheless great. Your letter was very interesting, being written almost on the eve of your becoming a Mother. You said how sweet it was of me to think about you in the midst of all my trials, but after thinking your letter over I rather feel that it should be vice-versa. Yours was a greater trial than any I will have to face, yet you managed to say how much you were thinking of me. So it is a mutual affection which I hope we will always hold on to whatever may happen.

In the good old days of our youth I suppose Syd and I used to 'gang' up on you, being the only girl, but since I have been away I know who has kept in my thoughts most between the two of you. It is very seldom that I hear from Syd, and yet no. 85 seem to get easily hurt because I address most of my letters to no. 9. I always try to make my letters interest them all, because I rarely get time or material to enable me to discriminate between everyone. Perhaps this life is hardening me a little too much, but I think I will need a mind of my own after the war is over, so it is probably a good thing.

I can imagine how hard it would be for you to see Mother go, but at best she was able to be present at the crucial period, and I know how proud our parents would be to be near the three of you. Anyway I trust Mike (sorry) is providing you both with plenty of happiness, and not too much trouble.

The three of us who left the ship together have passed our exams, so that news was a relief. Five in the class failed, which was rather a high proportion considering the time we all had to put into it. We are still waiting to see how and when we are going back to the old ship. At present we are having quite an easy time in here. I have an office job away from here, whilst the other two are engaged inside. There is plenty of spare time so I have been able to write, dhoby and read more freely than for many months. On the other hand, however, I will be glad to get back on the job.

We went ashore a couple of nights ago, had plenty to eat, and saw 'Gentleman Jim' on the films, which was right up our alley. Saturday should see us out again, as it is Ron's birthday.

I have just come across a Hunslet chap in here, and we had a good hours talk about Leeds in general, and Rugby football in particular. He was at Cockburn High School and had 5 credits and a good in his SC exams. I doubt whether we would have ever spoken to each other, had he not seen a cutting from the Yorks Post by my case as I was about to write to you.

I am keeping fit and reasonably happy now that I know my 6 weeks was not wasted. I trust you are both in good health also, and that John minor is not crying too much. Please give him a kiss from his Uncle John, though he will not appreciate who it is from for some time yet. Don't interest him in the Navy whatever you do or I will never forgive you!!!!! Cheerio for the present,

All the Best your affect brudder, John

20

FROM ACTION TO PASSENGER SHIP

THE DIARY (CONTINUED)

I soon settled down onboard once again with my old friends, and several new ones now that Bulldog and Ron had left us. My favourite, though one was never allowed to show favouritism, was a young Cockney named Murchison who was soon nick-named Shorty. I am only about 5 ft 8 ins and he did not reach up to my shoulders!! He was my second hand for some time, and was always trying to do something to help me in one way or another.

It was certainly a happy staff and life was quite pleasant. Whilst in *Canopus* my engagement had been broken off, but with good counsel from my friends, and a quick swallowing of pride, I realised it was probably for the best. Unfortunately it meant my mail was cut down by approximately one third.

On February 8th 1945, HMS *Aurora* left Alex. (thank goodness) for a trip to Suez through the ever-interesting canal once more. Hardly had we arrived, however, when the ship was recalled to Alex. again. All sorts of rumours were going around, the main being that Churchill and Roosevelt were to have conferences onboard. It was almost correct but not quite. A few of us were coming off shore early on Feb. 15th, and we found the jetty and ship surrounded by military police, detectives and even bloodhounds. Eventually we managed to get onboard, and, as I had the forenoon watch (8 to 12.30) I was in on all the excitement.

I was told to keep a vigilant watch seaward for the American cruiser *Quincy*, which was carrying two of the Big Three. It seemed that she would be anchoring a few cables away, and that Mr Churchill alone would be coming over to see our Captain for a few minutes, and he hoped to persuade the grand old man to say a few words to the ship's company.

Soon after 11 am the Admiral's boat was seen approaching, its main occupants being Mr Churchill, Sarah, Randolph[16] and Vice-Admiral Tennant. After a short conference with our Captain (and a drink) he accepted the invitation to say a few words. We all felt very proud that he should speak to us amidst all his tremendous work and worry. He looked fit but very tired, and remarked on the great war work achieved by the *Aurora*, and hoped we would soon be home with our dear ones.

Then we gave three sincere and hearty cheers for the war's greatest leader, and as his boat proceeded inshore all ships could be seen cheering him and he responded characteristically with the V sign. It was a day to remember for us all. We were only sorry not to catch a glimpse of the late President Roosevelt.

Obviously Churchill's visit was not mere curiosity on his part, and we soon realised why he had a short conference with Capt. Barnard. The next day we left Alex and proceeded to Port Said through the canal as far as Ismaillia. This was King Farouk's favourite resort, and was where we were to pick up King Ibn Saud of Saudi Arabia. He had been in conference with Churchill, Roosevelt and Farouk. It was the first time he had left his country and we were to transport him and his large staff back to his capital Jedda.

A special area was roped off on the port side of the upper deck for the flock of sheep which would be the Arabs' main meal onboard. A movable arrow was fitted on the quarter-deck, the use of which I will explain later, and living quarters for the King, his Cabinet ministers and servant were arranged.

On Feb 18th the party, containing sheep and much baggage, began to arrive. As the King was paralysed he had to be hoisted inboard. The moment he arrived onboard we broke the Arabian ensign at the fore and the King's personal standard at the main. The same day we sailed for Jedda.

The trip was only short and took less than 2 days. We watched the 'executioner' calmly killing sheep, our guns were fired to amuse the passengers, and twice a day they all prayed in the direction of Mecca, which was indicated by the aforesaid arrow. It was an experience the like of which can never have been equalled by a man-o-war. On Feb 20th we arrived at Jedda where the ship was soon surrounded by scores of gaily beflagged vessels of all shapes and sizes. Before leaving us, Ibn Saud left expensive presents for almost everyone onboard and many men became fully fledged sheiks!!! As he left the ship we fired a 21 gun salute, and hauled down the ensigns, one of which broke in half to our dismay.

---

16 Sarah and Randolph were Churchill's daughter and son.

The Captain was telling us on the bridge one night that the King had 37 wives, but was only allowed 4 at a time. Ain't it a shame!!! Goodness knows how many sons he had. I saw about a dozen.

On our return journey to Alex, we stopped at Ismaillia again, and gave a party onboard to WRNS who were keen to visit a famous fighting ship!!

On Feb 24th we arrived back in Alex once more and had almost a month in there for docking and repairs, plus a welcome rest.

21

I BECOME A YEOMAN, AND GENOA MAKES ME WORK FOR A LIVING

On March 23rd we sailed for Naples, and once again I left the ship for a short time. Ever since I passed for Ldg. Sig. (Higher) I had been acting as instructor for our staff, which should really have been the job of one of our two Yeomen. Then I heard that the other leading hand (we were hardly the best of friends as you may remember from previous chapters), had decided to take the exam for Yeoman (Lower Grade), the actual rate being VS2 (L) and rank of petty officer. This made me laugh as I had a very poor opinion of his ability, and the Chief suggested that if he was going in for it there was my chance also to see what I could do.

I told the Chief and also Lieut. Finlayson, our Signals Officer, that I had no interest in promotion if my demobbing would be delayed by it. (At that time prospects for Germany were not so bright.)

To cut a long argument short I was eventually persuaded to take the exam, chiefly because our Senior Yeoman was almost due to leave the ship, and I saw a chance of staying with my pals. (If I passed!!!) So, on April 10th, the other chap and myself went ashore to Fort Del Ovo or HMS *Byrsa II* at Naples. The ship was due to visit Leghorn for a few days, so a leading hand was sent to relieve us temporarily. We saw the ship sail the following day, and I settled down to a few days' study. The other chap was confident, and made fun of my swotting whilst he was stepping off ashore every night. I only went out once in the 5 days we spent in barracks. The chaps based ashore had a black market all their own with the local Italians. Cigarettes 6/- a packet, chewing gum 2/6, hair-cream 10/-, boots £3 or £4 and so on.

A leading hand from C in C Med's staff joined us for our exams. We commenced with oral, and I was very pleased with my efforts. This was followed by a full practical exercise of flashing, semaphore and Morse flag, plus two written papers. We commenced at 8 am and finished at 3.30 pm. This was April 16th, and on completion we returned to the *Aurora*, who had arrived during the day. I was having supper in the mess, when a messenger reported that the results were coming through by semaphore. I dashed up to the bridge and read Allen – failed, Dawson – passed etc., and that was that. I had no sympathy with Allen as he did not deserve it!!

We stayed at Naples a further week with a day trip to Sorrento to relieve the monotony. This was a pleasant little town and resort, which looked and smelled good. There were many orange groves, and one of 'our gang' stood on my shoulders in an endeavour to purchase a few. All he succeeded in doing was to dislodge a brick on to my head, and the rest of the day was hazy to me!!!

On April 24th we left Naples for Malta where we had one extremely busy day. As our next job was likely to occupy us for several weeks, several men due for relief were drafted off at short notice. Our staff especially underwent changes and Yeoman Boyd left with the other leading sig. and two signalmen. Reliefs came for all except the Yeoman. I was rated on the 26th April and therefore took his place. After a lot of persuasion from me Jim had taken an exam for leading sig. (Lower), which he successfully passed, so he became one of two new leading hands. So everything worked out very nicely for our gang, except that Laurie had left for England previous to all this, for compassionate reasons.

After a day at Naples again, we heard that our next job was to be in charge of a mixed force, which was to sweep and eventually approach and occupy Genoa in Northern Italy. With us we had several destroyers, a minesweeping flotilla, launches, torpedo boats, store and supply ships, bar vessels, tankers etc., so it looked like a busy time for our staff.

The first 10 days were spent some distance away whilst the sweepers viewed the scene. The weather was very rough at times, and on May 2nd I was one of the main actors in a realistic drama. I was on watch on the bridge in rather rough conditions, when Jim (on the flag deck below) told me there was a suspicious looking object ahead of us. Almost as soon as he told me I saw a dirty-looking, horny mine on top of a wave only a few feet from the bows. I shouted 'Mine just ahead, Sir,' and prepared for the explosion. The Navigator, however, was really alert and a marvellously cool alteration of course in the nick of time averted a major tragedy.

When the Captain came on the bridge he asked who had reported the mine and the Navigator said the look-out just behind me. I was so surprised I never said a word and he accepted the Captain's praise

John Dawson in his Yeoman of Signals uniform, 'A 'Pretty' Officer',
in 1948 at 7 Cliff Lane, Leeds.

without turning a hair. The whole business had been so short and dramatic, that I think the Navigator mistook our voices. Anyway I told the Chief later and he was not slow in amending the error. It certainly was a close shave, a little too close for my liking.

On May 10th it was decided to move up towards Genoa with minesweepers leading the way through the channel. All the time, the other Yeoman and I were working 4 on and 4 off day and night, and it was really tiring and rather a strain.

A heavy fog impeded operations for several hours, and our siren worked overtime looking after our 'flock'. It was a great relief when the fog lifted and the line was able to move slowly towards the outer harbour. Incidentally VE day on May 8th was already past, and I recall the day especially as rather a queer thing happened. Our Signal Officer and Navigator both seemed pleased with my work since commencing the Yeoman's job, and said so, suggesting also that I was now top-of-the-tree in my particular branch and should take a commission. I said they had hardly selected the right day to ask me, as home was my one thought at such a time. Taking a commission would mean leaving the best pals I ever had, it would mean starting at the bottom again, and most important of all, would delay my demobbing if the Jap war were to end suddenly. So I replied firmly, 'Thank you, but the answer is no.'

On the afternoon of May 10th the proposed anchorage was reached, and we had a very busy time telling each ship where to berth as they came in. The inner harbour was too dangerous to enter, due to mines, wrecks and other obstacles. The next few days were almost a nightmare to our staff. The rough seas meant continuous vigilance and on several occasions small ships had to be sent to inlets for shelter, whilst the larger ships sailed in convoy until the weather moderated sufficiently to anchor without dragging. Mines were regularly spotted and sunk by the vigilant coastal craft, and convoys of landing craft were detailed to sail from Leghorn with supplies and facilities to enable the re-opening of the port to proceed as rapidly as possible. The rough seas were a constant trouble and of the 12 landing craft to reach the beach in the first convoy, only two were left serviceable after one very bad night when the storm and fires caused havoc. Several chaps were killed and a court of enquiry had to be held ashore.

There had been little fighting in Genoa itself, as the patriots had seized the town before the arrival of the Fifth Army. When a landing jetty was eventually fixed up I had two runs ashore until dusk, and found the town quite prosperous and scarcely damaged at all.

Once things began to settle down, our main duty was to act as 'Father' to the other ships. We supplied food, cigarettes, oil etc., to the smaller ships until our stocks ran out, and on May 15th we returned to Leghorn for more stores. The following day saw us back at Genoa, and until the end of the month we had our hands full organising everything. We must have made and received hundreds of signals a day. Eventually the inner harbour was made serviceable enough to receive the smaller ships, and a shore-base was opened up to take charge of the port and sailings. This was what we had been waiting for and it meant our work was done. On June 1st, as at Toulon, we were relieved by HMS *Sirius* and sailed for Naples.

THE LETTERS (CONCLUDED)

Ldg. Sig. J R Dawson
D/JX 232329
27 Mess
HMS Aurora
c/o GPO London
15/3/45

Dear Eileen, John and Michael

Very many thanks for the 10/- and letter received yesterday. I wish you would not send money though, as I am quite OK these days. After all I never repay you in any way.

It's good to have a photo of 'Junior' and you can be sure I look after it. I quite appreciate the joke you sent, though it is probably on yours truly. I think I can still manage to connive a laugh, but it's not as quite as sincere as the 'Blenheim Follies' one I used to have. We were a pretty raw crowd in those days, but it was great fun. I wonder if I will continue my doubtful career as a comic after the war. If Betty and I had continued together I would probably have gone into a shell as regards this, and other activities. After seeing 'The Happy Breed,' I realise there is always a chance of us coming together again as long as one party keeps the love light burning. Now don't worry, I am not writing to her except for a parting fling. If anything should bring us together again it will have to be Old Mother Nature. So there!!!!

I was very amused with the conductor episode, and I should think everyone else was with the exception of the unhappy conductor. These rough Irish people!!! I hope it was not John who through (sorry threw) him orf.

At present life is rather quiet as we have not left ourselves much to do since we cleared the Med. (With a little help from others of course)? We are getting plenty of sleep which is a good thing. Laurie, who was the oldest member of 'our gang', is now on his way home on compassionate grounds plus the fact that he is one of the first for de-mobbing. Syd, yet another, is due to leave for UK shortly to transfer to the Marine Engineers, so that will only leave Jim and myself of the shore-going party. I have two letters from Bulldog, and by this time he should be on another ship. As far as our future is concerned we look like doing 'police' duties for some time before getting anywhere nice like England. I could think of plenty worse jobs. A rather big transferring of naval personnel to the Army seems likely in the near future, but it does not touch me either voluntarily or compulsory. Only one chap in our staff is affected under the compulsory side of it.

I recently received a letter from Peggy B. which came as rather a surprise. She mentioned that neither her Mother nor herself had seen or heard of Betty for sometime. My answer would in all probability confuse her more than ever. Serves her right, the little rascal. Never will I trust the female of the species again, or will I ??? I wonder.

Thanks, Michael for the whopping big kiss. I return the compliment twofold. I trust you are all in good health and that John is not working too hard these days.

I think that practically exhausts my lack of news, so I will say cheerio and all the best to one and all.

Your loving brother and Uncle, (!)

John

LDG. SIG. J.R. DAWSON,
D/JX 232329,
27 MESS,
H.M.S. AURORA,
C/O G.P.O. LONDON.
15/3/45.

Dear Eileen, John & Michael,

Very many thanks for the 10/- and letter received yesterday. I wish you would not send money though, as I am quite O.K. these days. After all I never repay you in any way.

Its good to have a photo of "Junior" and you can be sure I look after it. I quite appreciate the joke you sent, though it is probably on yours truly. I think I can still manage to conjure a laugh, but its not as quite as sincere as the "BLENHEIM FOLLIES" one I used to have. We were a pretty raw crowd in those days, but it was great fun. I wonder if I will continue my doubtful career as a comic after the war. If Betty and I had continued together I would probably have gone into a shell as regards this, and other activities. After seeing "THE HAPPY BREED," I realise there is always a chance of us coming together again as long as one party keeps the love light burning. Now don't worry, I am not writing to her except for a parting fling. If anything should bring us together again it will have to be Old Mother Nature. Do I there!!!!

I was very amused with the conductor episode, and I should think everyone else was with the exception of the unhappy conductor. Those rough Irish people!!! I hope it was not John who though (say there) him off.

At present life is rather quiet, as we have not left ourselves much to do since we leaved the MED. (With a little help from those of course). We are getting plenty of sleep in which is a good thing. Lawrie, who was the oldest member of "our gang", is now on his way home on compassionate grounds, plus the fact that he is one of the first for demobbing. Syd, yet another, is due to leave for U.K. shortly to transfer to the Marine engineers, so that will only leave Jim and myself of the above going party. I have two letters from Bulldog, and by this time he should be on another ship. As far as our future is concerned we look like doing "police" duties for some time before getting anywhere nice like England. I could think of plenty worse jobs. A rather big transferring of naval personnel to the army seems likely in the near future, but it does not touch me either of voluntarily or compulsory. Only one chap in our staff is effected under the compulsory side of it.

I recently received a letter from Peggy B. which came as rather a surprise. She mentioned that neither her Mother nor herself had seen or heard of Betty for some time. My drawer would in all probability confuse her more than ever. Serve her right, the little rascal. Never will I trust the female of the species again, or will I ??? I wonder.

Thanks, Michael, for the whopping big kiss, I return the compliment twofold. I trust you are all in good health and that John is not working too hard these days.

I think that practically exhausts my lack of news, so I will say cheerio & all the best to one & all.

Your loving brother & Uncle, (x)
John.

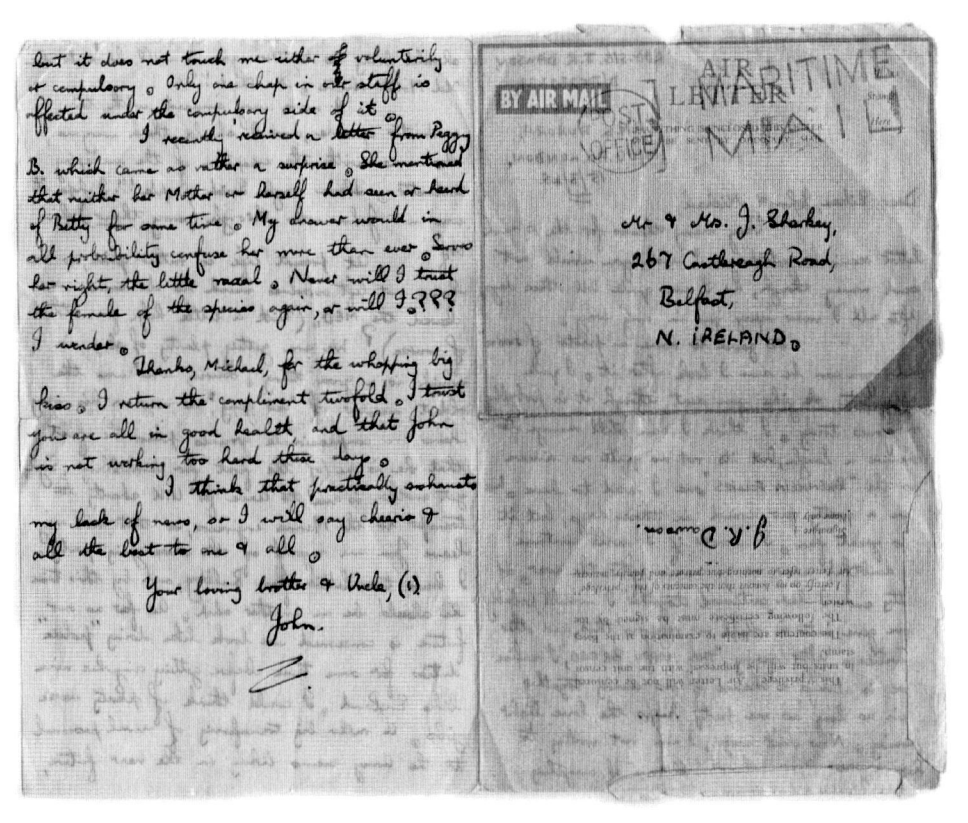

Mr & Mrs. J. Sharkey,
267 Castlereagh Road,
Belfast,
N. IRELAND.

Letter from John to Eileen & John & son Michael in Belfast dated 15th March 1945.

22

TROUBLE IN SYRIA, AND A WELCOME REFIT

THE DIARY (CONCLUDED)

On June 2nd 1945, we arrived at Naples, and were told to prepare to sail for Malta for our routine refit period. We had always been hoping to have a refit in UK, but the Captain said it was not likely so our hopes were never high.

Sunday morning, June 3rd, looked like being a nice quiet day and we were all dressed in our cleanest tropical rig. Whilst the majority of the ship's company were at Church, either onboard or ashore, I was duty Yeoman in the SDO. Suddenly an emergency signal was received asking how soon we could be ready to sail at 25 knots for an unknown destination. I immediately rushed the signal down to the Chief, who told me to take it without delay to the Captain at Church. It was not time for conscience and embarrassment, so I dashed into the recreation space during a hymn and showed the signal to the Captain. He followed me out, collected all the senior officers together, made many signals (oh, to be good at shorthand), received his sailing orders, and a few hours later we were off again.

We arrived at Alex the following afternoon, stored and ammunitioned ship, and continued to Beirut where trouble was brewing. Here we found our sister-ship HMS *Arethusa*, recently arrived in the Med. Vice-Admiral Tennant (Flag Officer Levant and Eastern Med) boarded us on June 6th, had several important meetings with Army generals and ambassadors, and on the 8th decided we could return to Alex.

We sailed about dusk, but an urgent signal was received about midnight and we returned to Beirut. Churchill had sent a message that a strong naval force was to remain at Beirut, and we had to remain until the arrival of HMS *Cleopatra* on the 9th. She duly arrived, we sailed for Alex, dropped the Admiral, and then headed to Malta at a slow 15 knots.

After all our recent exertions the next 3 days were like a cruise. The Captain was very sympathetic to our staff, and us two Yeomen were allowed to share our watches with the leading hands. This made life much easier, and I spent most of my time on the bridge in daytime wearing only white shorts and shoes. We were all full of joy at prospects of a spell in Malta, free from worry and strain.

One joke on this trip to Malta was worth remarking upon. A Cockney lookout was the comic in this case, and here roughly is his dialogue with the Officer of the Watch (OOW).

Lookout:-	Aircraft in sight bearing red 30, sir.
OOW (after slight pause):-	Are you sure it is not a star?
Lookout (sarcastically):-	If it is, sir, it's showing navigation lights!!!

We hardly passed a ship all the 3 days, and I had many interesting chats with Jim, various officers and look-outs on the bridge. As a leading-sig. I had never really felt in a position to speak to everyone freely, but success in my work as a Yeoman had given me confidence in myself, and others confidence in me. This is not idle boasting, but a fact which made me feel that any naval ambitions I had ever felt had been achieved.

We arrived at Malta on June 12th, in time to see HMS *Anson* sailing for the Far East. At least we knew there was no chance of us going in that direction, with so many new cruisers available.

23

FOUR MONTHS IN MALTA AND CRICKET

During our refit, which turned out to be much longer than planned, we had four spells in dry dock, the rest of the time being spent 'alongside the wall'. The weather was uncomfortably hot for docking, and practically all the ship's company had some ailment at one time or another. Sand-fly fever and skin diseases were the main trouble.

With peace time routine now the order in the Med, our ship's complement was reduced by over 100. Our staff lost one Yeoman and two signalmen. I was selected to remain onboard, much to my joy. Our Chief, who was group 10,[17] was due for demobbing but no reliefs were available in Malta, so Captain Barnard, who was due to go into hospital, asked me if I would take charge of the staff temporarily. He said he had confidence in me, so I said I would do my best. It was worth it if only to see how happy it made the Chief, and the tough chap we had always known broke down just before he left us. We hoisted the signal 'Cheerio' as he left the ship.

I actually had 3 weeks as Acting Chief, and after a pep talk to the staff, we determined to show the officers that a 'hostilities only' staff could be efficient and happy. In the sick absence of the Captain I had several tussles with our 'mad' Commander, but there were no bad mistakes. I had a cabin of my own and was monarch of all I surveyed. Eventually the new Chief arrived and I was only a plain Yeoman again!!!

To try and combat the sickness epidemic, the men were sent to various rest camps, varying from 4 days to a week. Some of the lucky ones went to Taormina and Messina, but I had to be satisfied with Ghain Tuffieha in Malta. The conditions were poor at this place as we lived in tents with flies, bugs, ants etc., but there was a lovely beach and I went swimming twice a day. I was 100% fit when I returned.

---

17 Demob groups were based on age and length of service, and determined a serviceman's priority for demobilisation.

I never had any illness at all during our 4 months, and I thanked my sport for that, chiefly cricket. We had a trial match against RNH Bighi. The Navigator was Captain, and the side looked quite strong. We won our first three games easily and I took 14 wickets. Our fourth match was against the best civilian team in Malta and we were well beaten. I did not want to play, as spinning the ball after so long out of the game had split open two of my fingers. I was made to play, however, with a bandaged hand. My bowling performance was 1 for 51, so I should never have played!!!

After our first few games, played on matting incidentally, several of the best men were drafted including two of the four officers in the team, including the Captain. Our Sports Officer could only play occasionally and it looked as if the team was going to die out, which would have been tragic. So I saw him, and my enthusiasm must have impressed, as I was given sole charge of the ship's cricket. I generally booked four grounds a week, and had inter-part games as well as challenging other ships. Although there were only 30 in our staff to pick from, the enthusiasm was terrific and they were fighting for places in the communications team. Only Nick Newman and I professed to be bowlers, whilst there were only 3 or 4 steady bats. Much to my amazement we won our first 6 games in great style. Our first inter-part defeat was on VJ+1 day, when some of the team had celebrated a little too much!!!

Altogether my communications team played 12 games, with 8 won and 4 lost. The ship played 16, won 9, lost 6 drawn 1. I played in all these games and also had the honour of playing in two representative games, once for the Rest v the Navy, and once for Ships in Harbour against Malta. My batting was spasmodic with 72 not out and 49 as best efforts, but I took about 111 wickets in these 30 games. We normally played clad only in white shorts, socks and shoes. It was a marvellous rig for cricket and I was like a nigger at the end of the season.

My happiest memory from 30 games?? Not my bowling, but when I amazed myself by scoring 72 not out. I usually batted number 9 or 10 in both ship and inter-part games. We were challenged by the flag-ship communications team in a 3-hour game, which meant approximately 85 minutes batting each. Our opening bat was unable to play and we knew the opposition was good. On winning the toss I was in a quandary, but decided to bat. I had hardly ever reached double figures in batting, so thought there would be nothing to lose if I went in first. I went in with our most reliable bat and we put 50 on the board before he was bowled. He had scored 42 (a brilliant effort), and I was 5. I was trying to play myself in for the first time in my life and although I had narrow 'squeaks' I stayed put. Other chaps came in and went out with useful 14's and 20's and then I had a go. I enjoyed every minute of it and when time was called we were 158 for 5 wickets and I was still there. The ovation I received was terrific, but I was like a furnace and had no strength left for bowling. I must have lost half a stone!!!

The opponents went for the bowling right away, and the two chaps I tried in my place had a bad time. I went on to bowl with the score 120 for 4, but could do little at first and they reached 140 for 5. Then I decided bold tactics were necessary if we were to win. I brought the field in and had six men close in to the bat. Then Nick and I put all we had into our bowling and intimidated them out. The last 5 wickets fell for 12 runs, and their last wicket fell in the last over with the score 152. It was the most exciting game I had ever played in and we were all thrilled by it.

Towards the end of the refit I had several games of football, which were enjoyable, but at which I showed no talent. Several of the staff, however, played in the ship's team.

During our time in Malta I met many old Navy pals including Mac and Bulldog. Mac was on his way home for demobbing, and Bulldog on his way to a job at Trieste.

Before we began working up again our old Captain was relieved by Capt. St. Vincent Sherbrooke VC DSO. He had only one eye and was a real successor to Nelson!!!

We were sorry to say goodbye to Captain Barnard, with whom we had gone through so much action. I personally had a great regard for him and the new chap did not compare at all favourably in my opinion.

24

WORKING UP AGAIN, A CRUISE, AND GOOD-BYE, *AURORA*

On October 20th HMS *Aurora* moved under her own steam for the first time in months, and sailed for Alex. to commence a working up spell again. This was all rather monotonous and the new Captain was very strict as regards dress at sea etc. and it did not go down too well. The difference between peace and war, which I knew would eventually irritate me, was showing itself from that time onward.

After a fortnight of gunnery, radar, communications, aircraft and other exercises we embarked Sir John Cunningham, the C in C Med., for a tour which he was wishing to carry out. The ship looked very smart after the refit, and a coat of paint made her look as good as new. Within the week commencing Nov 4th we visited Rhodes, Leros, Famagusta (Cyprus) and arrived at Haifa for Armistice Day.

Note:- Before leaving for the cruise with C in C I had a welcome night out in Alex. with Norman, now a Lieutenant, whom I had not seen for years. He arrived in Alex. on a Greek destroyer, saw the *Aurora*, and quickly contacted me. He was en route to a press job in Cairo, and we had a grand talk together.

I had a sightseeing tour of Rhodes (which we had bombarded 12 months previously), and our bus driver was a German prisoner. It was very interesting and the people were very much pro-Greek. Cyprus was hardly as enjoyable, though the difference in conditions between the New and Old town was remarkable. Ports, however, are pretty much the same anywhere and the saying 'A girl in every port' is not hard to believe, when one is continuously approached by small boys (and girls) asking 'Want a pretty girl etc.' It tended to become a nuisance to say the least.

There was quite a large naval force at Haifa, the Jewish immigration trouble being the cause. Armistice Day was very impressive and we all wore our full white suits for the inspection and ceremony. The bugler made the 'Last Post' a memorable period for us all. I had one run ashore in Haifa and it was a militant place at that time. A dusk curfew, and machine gun nests in the main streets made it all look rather impressive, but grim.

On 12th November we sailed with the flagship *Orion*, and the destroyers *Milne*, *Marne*, *Matchless*, *Stevenstone* and *Meteor* for a full day's exercises off Haifa. C in C Med, incidentally, left the ship before we sailed, as we were not returning. It was my first taste of peace time exercises with a fleet, but we 'muddled' through. Late in the evening all ships returned to Haifa, with the exception of *Aurora* and *Stevenstone* who proceeded in company to Alexandria.

We arrived in Alex on the 13th and then I had a marvellous shock, and what a shock. As duty Yeoman on the first night in harbour, I found we had scores of back signals to deal with.

As was the usual routine, any signals which were not straightforward were placed on one side for a quiet spell.

About 11 pm I began to sort out the queries, and found eventually that one of them referred to a signal, which we had not received, detailing an active service Yeoman by the name of Millnes to join *Aurora* vice Dawson, who was to be discharged to England on relief, on expiration of foreign service. I almost went mad then and spared no effort in tracing the missing signals from shore. There were 3 altogether, and I thought it must all be a dream. Jim, who had been my special pal for 2½ years, had mixed feelings. We had both expected that he would be sent home before me, owing to the shortage of Yeomen in the Med. Also he had recently refused a chance of release under Class B!!!

The next couple of days dragged horribly, but on the 14th Nov. my relief arrived. He was a real Navy man, and was a pensioner. He had volunteered for a further 12 months in the Med to be near his WREN sister, but had not bargained on a sea-going draft. It was his first sea-going ship for 6 years, so the Chief was not too happy about him when I left.

I stayed onboard until the 16th in order to tell him all the 'dope' and had a farewell night with all my pals the night before I left. My last morning onboard was one endless stream of 'Good-Byes', 'Good Lucks' and 'Lucky So and So's', and I had to pay visits to the Signal Officer's cabin, also the Navigator's, as well as the ratings' and petty officers' messes. It was all extremely awkward. I wanted to go and yet I didn't.

At 1.15 pm I left the ship, spent a few uncomfortable days under canvas in HMS *Sphinx*, proceeded by rail to Port Said on the worst railway system in the world, and 75 of us there joined HMS *Indomitable*, a carrier, as she steamed through the canal en route for Portsmouth. (Pompey to all men of the sea.)

We were accommodated in an aircraft hangar, 700 of us, and it was pretty grim. It was a 15-knot trip and after one night in Gibraltar on the way, we arrived in good old England on Friday, Nov 23rd, 1945. Relatives and friends by the hundred cheered and shouted as we entered Portsmouth Harbour, and there were not many of us who kept dry eyes. It was very moving, and we hardly felt the intense cold at first, amidst all the other excitement.

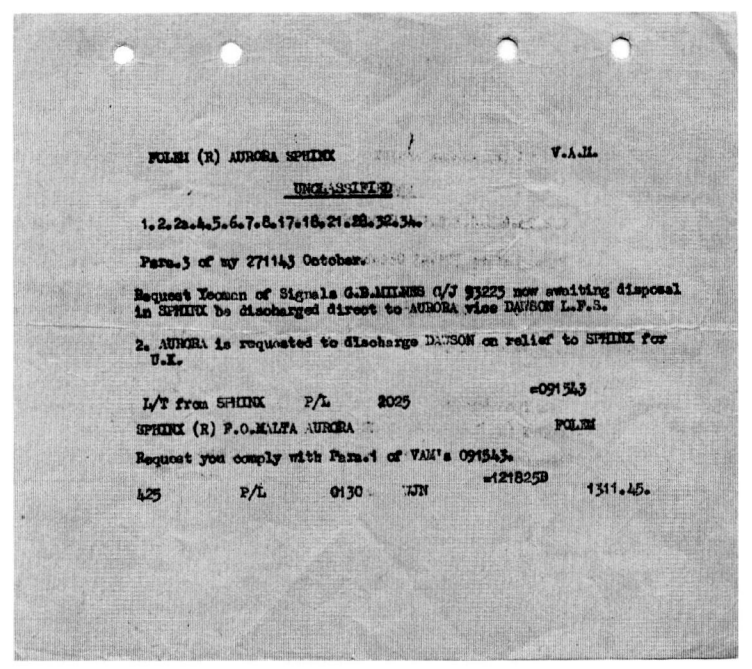

Signal to HMS *Aurora* for discharge of John Dawson from service.

25

THE LAST EPISODES, BEFORE BECOMING MR DAWSON

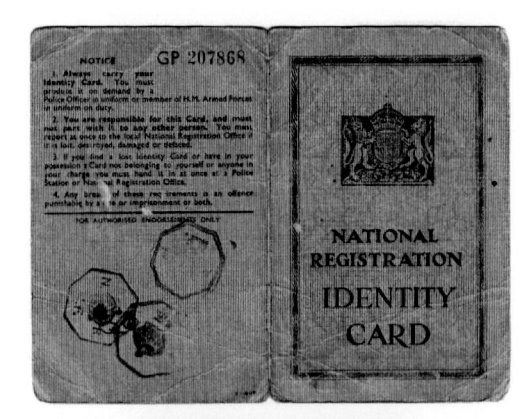

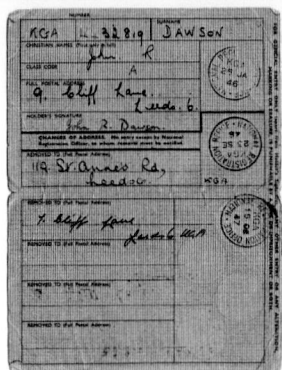

John Dawson's ID card 1946-47.

My home base was Devonport, so along with some 150 others I left the *Indomitable* the following morning in a special train. Most of the party were due for demobbing, only 3 of us home for length of foreign-service. We spent Saturday night sleeping on the floor or deck of the gymnasium after having been given instructions for the following day. I had a cold night and lost no time in being around early on Sunday morning. My only thought was to get on Leave as soon as possible.

I saw the regulating Chief Yeoman at 8.30 am and found he knew our former Chief Yeoman of *Spartan* and *Aurora*. This was a good start and he said he would get me on leave by dinner time. I had to visit Sick Bay, Victualling, Pay, Regulating, Mess and Baggage offices and it was a hard job on a Sunday, when no one was very helpful. When all this had been done the Chief saw the Duty Officer, and I proceeded on 46 days' foreign service and survivor's leave about noon.

I arrived home early Monday morning, and it was a marvellous feeling to see my parents and a nice, soft bed plus pyjamas. The leave was an enjoyable one. I was surprised at the new faces at Blenheim, pleased at the enthusiasm instilled by Mr Williams,[18] gratified at the sincere welcome with which I was received both at the firm and at Blenheim. I became very friendly with Lewis Duggleby, ex-RN, and his company became a god-send to me amongst all the new faces and absent ones. My premature demob party was a source of great joy, but I felt strangely humble at the kind thoughts expressed by many. I did not feel worthy of them, as I am well aware of my shortcomings.

On the female side I made a point of seeing Betty, but the reaction was NIL, for which I was thankful. At Blenheim I was glad to see old friends such as Grace, Peggy and Pearl, plus new ones such as Mollie, Sheila and Margaret.[19] I felt strange for some time, but not due to any lack of friendliness on the part of others.

I realised I was missing the male company to which I was so accustomed, and my nights with Mac (whom I looked up at Bradford), and Lewis, were invaluable to me. Mac and I also had a happy weekend at Blackpool with Laurie at his private hotel.

I had a happy week at Belfast with sister Eileen, and fell in love with nephew Michael just as easily as I had with Carol and Richard[20] in Leeds. Yes, it was a happy six weeks, my only trouble being that I had to be doing something all the time to keep my mind occupied. My dear Mother and Father were no doubt more than worried at my occasional unsettledness, but I think the reaction was only to be expected.

I settled down so well on this leave, that I returned on Jan 15th 1946 feeling miserable and wondering how long my demobbing would be. To my surprise I went to St Budeaux demob centre on Jan 17th and became a civilian on Wednesday Jan 23rd. I met many old friends on this last week, and had the company of another 'hostility' Yeoman, the only one I had ever met.

---

18 The new Church minister.
19 Mollie later became Mrs John Dawson.
20 Carol and Richard were Sydney and Kathleen's first two children.

Conditions at the demob centre were grim, which made one only too glad to get away from the Navy and its bad side. My one regret was that Jim arrived in barracks the day I left and I missed him. Since then, however, a meeting has been arranged with Laurie, Mac and Jim.

Well then, I arrived home early Thursday morning with a great load off my mind, but with many happy memories of a job done to the best of my ability. A week of leave and I began work in an endeavour to pick up the lost threads.

What did the Navy do to me? It gave me experiences which will provide life-long memories, some good, others bad. It provided me with a broader outlook on life, and my fellow men in particular. I found sincere friendships with all sorts of chaps, and achieved much more confidence in myself. For good things gained there are inevitably a few not so good, but my conscience is clear that I have not professed to be what I am not. What of the future? I have my ambitions and hopes, but time alone will help to sort them out and at the same time sort a few personal problems of my own.

SO ENDS THIS ROUGH NARRATIVE OF 61 MONTHS IN THE ROYAL NAVY

J R Dawson
Wed. March 20th 1946

LIFE AFTER THE WAR

As mentioned late in his Diary, a young woman called Mollie was now attending Blenheim Church. Dad married Mollie on 14th September 1946. Initially they lived at Mollie's mother's house in St Annes Road, Headingley, Leeds, along with Mollie's Grandfather Shaw. I was born to them on 7th September 1947 and my sister Pat on 6th August 1948.

The Wedding of John and Mollie Dawson on 14th September 1947 at Blenheim Baptist Church, Leeds, and then at Castle Grove, Headingley, Leeds. Front left are John's parents and front right his brother, Sydney. Just on his right and behind are Mollie's mother and grandfather. To John's right are his best man and friend, Norman Brooks, and to his right is Lewis Duggleby who had also served in the Royal Navy and joined Blenheim Church after the War.

By the time Pat came along my parents were living at 7 Cliff Lane, next door to Dad's parents and next door but one to my Great Uncle and Aunt (Robert and Lena Gawler).

Dad was working at John Dawson & Son, the family brush manufacturing business, near the centre of Leeds. Mum and Dad continued to be active at Blenheim Church. All our early holidays were held in Blackpool or St Annes. There was not a lot of money about. We had no car until the early 50s and no television until late 1953.

All the immediate family now lived in Headingley. Dad's brother Sydney and his wife Kathleen had three children – Richard, Carol and Stephen. Eileen and John lived in St Michaels Lane alongside Headingley Stadium, the home of Leeds Rugby League and Yorkshire Cricket, with their sons, Michael and Peter.

S. 1586 (A). (Established—November, 1944.)

ORDER FOR RELEASE FROM NAVAL SERVICE (CLASS A)
(MEN)

H.M.S. ....

To DAWSON, J.R. .... (Name)   (Date) .... 194...
                                         (See Note 1.)
.... YEO. S.(R.S). .... (Rating)

Official Number JX. 232329

1. You are being released from Service, by order made under authority of the Naval and Marine Forces (Temporary Release from Service) Act, 1940, as a Class A Release. (See Note 2.)

2. The date of your Release will be 28·3·46 .... 194...

   *Delete this line if no foreign service leave has been granted.

3. You have been granted leave as follows, starting on the day after the date of this Order :—
   *X days' foreign service leave expiring on .... 28·3·46 .... and 66 days' resettlement leave expiring on the date of your Release.

4. You are free to take up civil employment at any time after the date of this Order.

5. You may wear civilian clothing while on leave, and you are to cease to wear uniform after the date of your release.

6. After your release you will be regarded as being in Reserve and you will be liable until the end of the present emergency to recall to the Naval Service by revocation of this Order at any time. You will not be recalled, however, except in extreme emergency. (See Note 3.)

7. Your home address is noted in official records as follows ....
   9, Cliff Lane, Leeds 6, Hyde Park ....

   You are to report all changes to the Commodore of your Depot (if a Royal Naval Reservist to the Registrar General, Shipping and Seamen, Llantrisant Road, Llandaff, Cardiff; if a Royal Marine to the Commandant of your Division). While you are on leave you should also report any changes of address to the Officer in Charge of the Pay Office from which you were paid.

8. Your Service Certificate will be sent to you after your Release.

9. You should carry this Order with you until your Service Certificate is received and you are to produce it when required.

                                          ....
                                (Rank) ....
                                              Commanding Officer.

NOTES.

NOTE 1.—This date is the date on which the rating leaves his ship or establishment.

NOTE 2.—Class A consists of individuals released from the Forces under the Plan for Re-allocation of Manpower during the interim period between the defeat of Germany and the defeat of Japan, in priority of age and length of war service.

NOTE 3.—This release does not affect the normal liability of Pensioners to further service nor of Reservists (who are so liable under the Naval Forces (Extension of Service) Act, 1944) to further service or training.

C.W. 47163/44.

(8/8/45) (671) Wt. 27449/D8108 500M 9/45 S.E.R. Ltd. Gp. 671

John Dawson's Order for Release from Naval Service 1946.

We spent a lot of time together as a family and we all attended Blenheim Church and Sunday School. In 1953, we all settled down in front of a small television screen (in a large cabinet) at Grandpa and Grandma's at 9 Cliff Lane to watch the Coronation. This was the only TV in the family at that time. I remember it rained, but nevertheless the youngsters, bored with the Coronation, went out into Cliff Lane to play 'touch and pass'.

Early in my life, Dad started to take me to see Leeds Rugby home matches at Headingley. We would walk there together via his sister Eileen's home at 61 St Michael's Lane, where we would have a glass of home-made (non-alcoholic) ginger wine, and Michael, Peter and I would cross the road to the Boys' entrance queue. We stood at the front in the corner behind the goalposts; Dad stood further back with his friend Archie Wood (also from Blenheim).

Dad also took me to Headingley in the summer to watch Yorkshire and England play cricket. In those days Yorkshire only played a few games there, as their games were spread around the county, at Bradford, Sheffield, Harrogate, Middlesbrough and Scarborough. Even before that, we'd occasionally miss Sunday School and Dad would take us to Roundhay Park arena to watch Sunday games with the Bob Appleyard XI and other such teams.

The biggest game Dad and I ever attended was probably the first day of the England v. Australia Test in August 1977 when Geoffrey Boycott scored his 100th first class 100. However, we saw big games and big names well before that – Hutton, Washbrook, Trueman, Statham amongst others.

Back to Blenheim. I remember Dad being Church Secretary, an important post at a Baptist Church. One of the Deacons, he was responsible for the conduct of Church meetings and Deacons' meetings. I recall when Blenheim was without a Minister and we had a potential new Minister visiting for a 'sample' Sunday. Mum, Dad, Pat and I with another Deacon, had driven up to Barrow-in-Furness the previous Sunday to hear the Minister preach at his own Church. When he came to Blenheim he was good, but at his own Church he was dull, as we reported back later.

The system is that a Minister visits, preaches and is interviewed by the Deacons. They then make a report and recommendation to a Church meeting (a meeting of all Church members) and a majority of three quarters of those voting has to be achieved.

In this case, as a result of the report of our visit to his Church, the requisite majority was not attained.

As can be seen, Church was at the centre of our family's life. Pat and I went to Brownies and Cubs and then Guides and Scouts respectively at Church, as did our cousins. Uncle Sydney was Scoutmaster. As we got to our teens, we all went to the Church Youth Group, run by Dad and Mr Davidson. There were probably about 30 or more of us there growing up together. The Dawson family was at the centre of things.

Reprinted from
"BRUSHES"
356-358 Kilburn High Road, London, N.W.6
January, 1949

The male workers of John Dawson & Son in 1948 with John on the right in overalls in front of his father. This appeared in an 80th Anniversary brochure produced by the firm.

A Famous Brush House

C. BENNETT   F. W. DAWSON   H. S. DAWSON   J. R. DAWSON   D. S. DAWSON

DAWSON'S
Largest Manufacturers of Machine Brushes in Yorkshire

The Dawson's management team in 1948 from the same brochure.

Obviously the other part of Dad's life continued to be the family brush business, with his brother Sydney and second cousin Clifford Bennett (another Blenheimite!). It was a partnership at that stage. Its factory was near the centre of Leeds and was old, and old-fashioned, but full of character. However, it stood in the way of the proposed Leeds Inner Ring Road, and in due course the works was moved to a new building at the West Park Ring Road, nearer to where Mum and Dad had moved to live in 1967. The works is still there today, but more of that later.

Dad was on the national industry wage negotiating committee as an employer, and I recall meeting him off the London train, with Mum, at the old Leeds Central Station on Wellington Street, with its wonderful smoky smells from the steam engines. He used to travel with the union shop steward from Dawson's to those meetings.

In 1968, Dawson's celebrated its Centenary with a big dinner at the Metropole Hotel in Leeds, which I attended.

Unfortunately, Clifford Bennett died in his 50s of a heart attack on his way to sing in the choir at an evening event at Blenheim Church, which we were all at. The dramatic news came through during the evening. This caused issues for the business and the risks of a partnership as a business structure were seen. The business changed to a limited company after this – Dawson & Son Limited.

John Dawson outside the premises of Dawson & Son Limited at West Park Ring Road, Leeds to which the business had moved in late1970.

Dad never wanted me to go into the business. He and Mum were determined I should be well educated and develop my own career. In 1955, I began at Leeds Grammar School, then a direct grant school. I stayed till 1966. My cousins, Michael and Peter Sharkey and John Bennett (Clifford's son), also attended LGS. Dad did not believe a small independent family business had a long-term future. Major competitors like Harris and Addis were growing and buying up businesses. He was wrong as it turned out. These big companies wanted assembly-line procedures. Dawson's was a specialist manufacturer that did not fit their desires. It actually prospered as time went on. Dawson's was sold to a Dutch family business in 2005 when the two remaining directors were approaching retirement with no successors.

Dad became a Magistrate in Leeds in the 60s and loved this new and different role. He sat on Tuesdays, and in those days the courts were sitting in Leeds Town Hall.

Mum and Dad were always Conservatives that I can recall, paying their subscriptions to NW Leeds Conservatives. The first political meeting I went to was with Dad at either the 1964 or 1966 election to hear Keith Joseph speak at an election meeting in Woodhouse, part of his NE Leeds constituency. We lived in Cliff Lane then, where our side of the street was in NW Leeds and the other side in NE Leeds.

So began my interest in Conservative politics, leading to my being a parliamentary candidate twice, a local council candidate a few times and for a short spell, a County Councillor.

Dad lived to see all my campaigns and see me qualify as a solicitor and teach as a Polytechnic Lecturer in Leeds. However, he did not live to see me get a 'proper job', as he would have called it, at Skipton Building Society; first as in-house Lawyer and eventually as Secretary & General Manager.

He lived to see me marry twice. He saw Pat marry and have two children. Once Mum and Dad had finished paying for school fees for Pat (at Leeds Girls High School) and me, they were able to travel more abroad. They visited many of the places Dad had seen in the War – Malta, Gibraltar, Crete, but their favourite places were Cyprus and Jersey, where they spent many holidays.

When the Cyprus troubles began between the Greek Cypriots and the Turkish, Mum and Dad were on holiday in Famagusta and Dad was also doing business with a customer between there and Nicosia. Dad did not often send postcards; he left it to Mum. This time he wrote, saying weather and hotel good. 'Unfortunately, can't go out at night because of the curfew, can hear machine guns in the street. See you soon.'

Subsequently his customer's factory was destroyed in the fighting and Famagusta came under Turkish control. They moved their holiday destination to Limassol.

In 1985 Dad sat down with me one day and talked about the sinking of the *Spartan* in 1944. He explained that he had swapped duties with a signalman, so Dad was on the bridge and the other chap was on the rear bridge, when the ship was hit. He had been bored with the rear duty. As a result he lived and the other chap died. Dad said that he and others got through the war with the view that if your number was up, that was it. His number was not up.

Dad smoked all his life. I can recall the cigarettes initially being John Players and Senior Service (untipped). I suspect this habit may have helped shorten his life. Dad died on 3rd May 1986, aged 64. It was Rugby League Cup Final Saturday. Mum and Dad had been to Harrogate in the morning. Dad had complained of indigestion when they got home. He went to bed, but went downstairs to watch the Cup Final before going back to bed.

When Mum could not wake him later she rang Pat and she and her husband Stuart rushed round to try to help. Pat rang me and we rushed across from our home in Keighley. It was too late. He had died.

Fortunately, I had seen Dad on the previous Wednesday evening. I called in on my way home from work in Leeds. He was working on Magistrate's business. Mum was not at home but had left him a casserole for his tea. He looked grey but said he was okay, just tired.

Dad was a wonderful man, loved by his family and liked by everyone. He served his community, his Church, his workpeople and colleagues. He was an ordinary man who also served his country as a naval signalman, as shown in this book.